EFFECTIVE FAMILY OFFICE

EFFECTIVE FAMILY OFFICE

Best Practices and Beyond

Angelo Robles

Effective Family Office: Best Practices and Beyond describes how the most innovative and successful single family offices (SFOs) respond to a turbulent world, uncertain economy, threats from cyber and terrorist attacks, constantly evolving regulations, tax structures and risks, as well as challenging family dynamics and unprecedented rates of wealth creation.

Author Angelo Robles, founder and CEO of Family Office Association and Effective Family Office, identifies the most effective tools, policies, procedures, and elements of family and organizational culture that new and existing SFOs must embrace to achieve and maintain excellence. "It all boils down to people," Robles says. "'Effective,' 'Resilient' and 'Adaptive' are the three building blocks of stunning SFO success: finding effective people, managing them to embrace a resilient mindset, and creating an adaptive culture."

"The single family office (SFO) community has reached its inflection point. It is eminently clear that SFOs sit in a commanding seat as they bear witness to history's greatest transition of family wealth taking its slow but inevitable path. The influence that SFOs can (by their role) and should (by its mandate) exert, could in many ways help preserve, protect, and serve the emerging generational beneficiaries, yet far too many 'catbird-sitting' SFOs remain woefully out of position to sufficiently do so. We're truly facing a massive conundrum: the stakes for families won't likely ever be higher!"

— DANA A. GREEN, FOUNDING PARTNER, SAGE STRATEGY PARTNERS

Dedication

*To my loving and ever supportive wife, Maria,
and our son, Dylan*

In the memory of my mother Silvia Robles

Table of Contents

E fficiency is overrated in the business world.

There, I said it!

After all, who cares how efficient your policies and procedures, technology and communication systems if they don't enhance your long-term, sustained success? In fact, by focusing on efficiency rather than effectiveness, many leaders only end up more efficiently leading their organizations down the wrong path.

This book reflects my synthesis and analysis of what I have been privileged, as founder and CEO of the Family Office Association, to learn from iconic families, inspired single family office executives, and top thought leaders and leading-edge experts in a variety of disciplines. In these pages, I describe the characteristics of the most innovative, resilient and successful SFOs—from family and company culture to policies and practices—that elevate them above mediocrity.

While a number of wealth management firms call themselves family offices, this book focuses on the single family office (SFO)—a privately owned and run firm developed for one family. Each SFO is as unique as the family it serves. As the saying goes: "If you've seen one single family office, you've seen one single family office."

Interest in SFOs has grown during the last 20 years, in response to a growing wave of worldwide wealth creation coupled with the global economic turmoil of the past decade. Banking and business failures, extreme economic and market volatility, and investment fraud have motivated many families of significant wealth to assume tighter control of their financial affairs to preserve their family legacy.

Some family office advisors say families should create an SFO once the family's total assets reach $50 to $100 million. Other advisors peg the threshold at $500 million or more. A more useful question to ask would be: Is my family's wealth—in all its financial and non-financial forms—being well served by my existing uncoordinated, sometimes conflicted advisory team?

SFOs generally offer the families they serve more than wealth advisors can or do provide. Depending on the size and complexity of the family's resources, SFO services can vary widely. SFOs coordinate and oversee various types of investment-related services, such as accounting, tax planning and compliance, asset protection and risk management, as well as personal family services. Most importantly, families want their SFO to preserve their dynastic wealth and reduce risks—including geopolitical instability, digital threats, catastrophic natural disasters or the collapse of a banking system, for example. (Appendix A itemizes many such services by category.)

Wealth X's "UHNW Report 2015-2016" estimates that, worldwide, there are approximately 212,615 ultra-high net-worth (UHNW) families with at least $30 million in financial assets, excluding collectibles, consumables, consumer durables and primary residences. The Family Office Association estimates that currently there only about 3,000 SFOs around the world, not counting quasi-family offices: small private family investment companies or family offices embedded within family-owned and-managed businesses. Given the number of UHNW individuals, why are there so few SFOs?

Reasons include lack of awareness of and education about the benefits of an SFO, fear of the complexity and potential cost of set-up and management, challenges in hiring capable staff, and lack of professional guidance.

But families that forego an SFO—whether by conscious decision or lack of awareness—are vulnerable to a host of troublesome issues, particularly in times of turmoil. For instance, these families often have fragmented and uncoordinated relationships with multiple banks, wealth managers and other business, investment and personal service providers. What's more, families pay high fees for this disorganized web of overlapping services. Worse, those fees likely are not fully disclosed, making it impossible to quantify or compare them, or effectively negotiate with service providers. Furthermore, many of the institutions they work with have built-in conflicts of interest. Brokers and other client-facing staff often receive higher commissions for selling the institution's own investment products, giving them an incentive to push these products rather than choose the product that best suits the client's needs and circumstances. Families rarely have the staff or the expertise to vet investment advisors or individual investment opportunities, heightening the chances that they may inadvertently enter into a subpar investment, or even a Ponzi scheme or other fraud.

Now more than ever, wealthy families need to coordinate their business, investment and personal relationships by centralizing management and oversight, implementing appropriate due diligence and risk management procedures, and managing their family affairs more effectively. For a family of significant wealth, an appropriately structured and well-run SFO may be the answer.

Successful families and exceptional SFOs both emphasize principles that enable generational families and their SFOs to thrive. These principles require talent, motivation, adaptive leadership and exceptional people, as well as progressive and innovative culture and processes.

Unfortunately, this is not how most SFOs operate. Mediocrity is accepted. Few families position the SFO to succeed with champion leaders who hire amazing employees, manage them to greatness, or provide them with the resources needed for tremendous success. If you're building or looking to strengthen an SFO, then why not build, reboot or restructure it to own the desired outcome: the delivery of world-class services that you and your family value most?

I have found that, in a nutshell, success boils down to people: finding effective people, managing them to embrace a resilient mindset, and creating an adaptive workplace around them. To be effective requires a family office not only to take advantage of new technology, but also create a culture of trust, superb communication, and shared purpose. As crucial as it is to keep up with technology, cultural advantage beats technical advantage, hands-down.

Winning culture requires being resilient. To be resilient requires "the capacity of a system to absorb disturbance and still retain its basic function and structure," say environmental scientists Brian Walker, Ph.D., and David Salt in their book "Resilience Thinking: Sustaining Ecosystems and People in a Changing World" (Island Press, 2006). The authors explain, "Humans are great optimizers. We look at everything around us, whether a cow, a house, or a share portfolio, and ask ourselves how we can manage it to get the best return. Our modus operandi is to break the things we're managing down into their component parts, understand how each part functions and what inputs will yield the greatest outputs ... [but] the more you optimize elements of a complex system of humans and nature for some specific goal, the more you diminish that system's resilience ... Resilience thinking is the inverse of predictive hubris. It is based in a humble willingness to 'know that we don't know' and 'expect the unexpected.'"

Similarly, retired General Stanley McChrystal and the co-authors of "Team of Teams: New Rules of Engagement for a Complex World" (Portfolio, 2015) explain, "In complex environments, resilience often spells success, while even the most brilliantly engineered fixed solutions are often insufficient or counterproductive." They point out that resilience is being studied in fields as disparate as psychology and hydrology, as well as in the business world. "In a resilience paradigm, managers accept the reality that they will inevitably confront unpredicted threats; rather than erecting strong, specialized defenses, they create systems that aim to roll with the punches, or even benefit from them." (Portfolio: 2015)

McChrystal points to investor and writer Nassim Taleb's concept of an "antifragile system" that is not easily damaged by shocks. "Robust systems weather shocks; and antifragile systems, like immune systems, can benefit from shocks." As Taleb writes in "Antifragile: Things That Gain from Disorder" (Random House Trade Paperbacks, 2014), "Our urge to specialize, reap efficiencies, and impose our demands for unnatural predictability has, like the rerouting of the Rhine, created new threats and damaged our ability to bounce back."

Taleb takes resilience a step further and posits, "Antifragility is beyond resilience or robustness. The resilient resists shocks and stays the same; the antifragile gets better ... The antifragile loves randomness and uncertainty, which also means—crucially—a love of errors, a certain class of errors. Antifragility has a singular property of allowing us to deal with the unknown, to do things without understanding them—and do them well." In fact, he writes, "I'd rather be dumb and antifragile than extremely smart and fragile."

From these definitions we understand that to be adaptive, processes and culture cannot be rigid, especially in a world that is changing ever faster and more furiously. The key here is culture, and the heart of culture is people. It's the people in an SFO who ensure that it is resilient and ready to face any challenge. The best way to allow for the highest resiliency is ensuring that the people who make up your culture are themselves flexible and prepared for a variety of challenges. SFOs would be much better at adapting if they were to hire a more diverse workforce of individuals of varying cultural backgrounds, ages and genders. The typical staff dominated, from top down, by male, well-entrenched and non-diverse employees, will find it challenging to create or maintain exceptional SFOs in a world that is diverse and ever-changing.

This book details steps that wealthy families can take to define their goals, which their SFO can parlay into progressive principles, exceptional hires, adaptive culture and world-class performance.

Chapter 1 presents the ingredients of an effective SFO; this information is designed for families that have yet to create or professionalize a family office. In Chapter 2, such families will also find useful information about how family governance structures can help family members work effectively with each other and their family office. Chapter 3 deals with the ideal traits of family office CEOs and how they can provide effective top-down management of staff. Chapter 4 addresses ownership of outcomes, adapting and embracing disruption.

Maintaining a learned mindset, the value of perpetual learning and asking constant questions are the purview of Chapter 5.

Chapter 6 focuses in on filling the talent bus, overlooked hiring criteria, creating a talent pipeline, dynamics diversity among employees, defining roles and understanding your employees needs.

Family office leaders need to understand and honor the unique culture of the family, and create an SFO culture that will be resilient enough to not only deal with, but benefit from, constant changes in the family and the outside world. Chapter 7 describes the lessons SFO and family leaders can learn from the corporate world about the importance of culture, as well as strategies for defining and building a brand—one that creates an exciting and positive experience for family members and helps the SFO respond to the family's evolving needs.

Chapter 8 covers how a family's heritage can inform the ways its SFO evolves over time, as the family changes and grows. Chapter 9 describes how superior SFOs can enhance the way they manage the family's investments and finances. It includes an investing primer and also covers global custodianship, private trust companies and a strong back office.

With a special emphasis on technology, including artificial intelligence, machine learning and virtual reality, Chapter 10 helps family offices get up to speed on technology, while pointing out ways to mitigate many potential risks in the digital world. I wrap up with my closing comments in the final section titled conclusion.

Appendix A presents an exhaustive list of SFO services that families may want to consider exploring with their SFO executives.

My hope is that families will use what they can from this book to form or transform their family office into a truly world-class, effective organization that meets their evolving needs and wants.

1

Ingredients of an Effective SFO

The influence that SFOs can (by their role) and should (by their mandate) exert, could in many ways help preserve, protect, and serve the emerging generational beneficiaries, yet far too many catbird-sitting SFOs remain woefully out of position to sufficiently do so. We're truly facing a massive conundrum: the stakes for families won't likely ever be higher!"

— DANA GREEN, D. GREEN AND ASSOCIATES

Many SFOs are mediocre at best and woefully inefficient at worst. They miss the excellence mark by a long shot. They descend into mini-bureaucracies, fall behind the innovation curve, and have difficulty attracting and retaining exceptional talent.

Classically defined, SFOs centralize, preserve and transfer significant dynastic wealth across generations. They act as an effective inter-generational safeguard and touchstone for the family's collective values, aspirations, heritage and legacy. However, providing these and other services is not what makes an SFO world-class.

These are simply deliverables that the family requests of its SFO. To truly understand what the formation of (or transformation to) a world-class organization looks like, we must start at the beginning.

FORMING A TASK FORCE

Families that want to form or improve an SFO should start by pulling together a task force made up of family leaders to spearhead the planning effort. Families can consider tapping long-time trusted advisors to participate on the task force, but a word of caution: Conflicts of interest or loyalty to the older generation or one branch of the family may cloud their objectivity or threaten their position with the family. Choose your task force carefully and consider any underlying motivations that may affect the attitudes or direction provided by your advisors. Families without a family office would be advised to rely on one experienced "quarterback" SFO specialist to help galvanize this effort, adding more specific specialists as needed. As a group, the task force should decide:

- *Who are the SFO's clients?* Make a list of everyone to be served by the SFO, such as individuals, family branches, investment entities, businesses, trusts, trust companies and foundations. The design of the SFO should take into account each client's unique needs and requirements.
- *Which assets will be managed by the SFO?* List all the types of assets that the SFO will be responsible for managing: marketable securities, hedge fund interests, MLPs, direct investments, operating businesses, residential real estate, commercial real estate, farms, collections, aircraft, yachts, horses, sports teams, etc.
- *Which services do the clients of the SFO need and want?* Families with extensive investments, or with liquid capital to be invested, will need investment management services including development of investment policy statements and asset allocation plans, manager due diligence, and investment reporting. All SFO clients need comprehensive and accurate performance reporting and accounting and tax-return preparation. Another nearly universal need of SFO clients is the coordination of risk management, security and reputation management. Development and coordination of estate and tax planning is an obvious need of a multi-generational client group, but can be equally critical for a first-generation entrepreneur who wishes to perpetuate the family's legacy over the long term.

    Other possible needs include property management and staffing, bill payment and concierge services—which can include managing physical assets (such as homes, cars, a yacht and private jet) and vetting domestic help, nannies, private schools and summer camps.

2

- *What will the SFO's business plan look like?* It should outline the services to be provided, a short-and long-term timeline, necessary talent (employee and outsourced), service partners required (e.g., custodians, tax counsel, security services) and technology needs.

  Dan Sullivan, co-owner of The Strategic Coach Inc. and one of the world's top coaches for entrepreneurs, teaches that looking at our businesses quarter by quarter is often far more powerful and effective than creating three-year or five-year plans. Yes, long-term goals and plans are valuable. But in today's world, effectiveness, resilience and adaptability also require creating goals with much shorter time frames.

  A key objective of any business plan should be determining a budget. Typically, SFO budgets are defined as a percentage of assets under management. SFO operating costs vary widely—smaller SFOs, or those managing complex assets, tend to cost a greater percentage of their assets to operate than larger SFOs, or those managing a simpler portfolio, because there are fewer economies of scale to exploit. For example, the budget of an SFO managing an extensive and complex portfolio for three generations of family members, all of whom also share a passion for modern art and house their collections in multiple homes around the world, will necessarily be larger, both as an absolute number and as a percentage of assets under management, than the budget of an SFO managing a portfolio of publicly-traded securities for a single family unit.

  SFOs are expensive to operate; family members who will be paying the future bills may initially balk at the projected cost. However, when compared to the current expense of managing the family's assets—taking into consideration all costs, fees and expenses—the expense of an SFO will likely be lower. Because the SFO will be custom-tailored to the family's needs, the return on that expenditure will certainly be higher. The budget will drive the creation of benchmarks to set expectations for SFO performance.

- *How will the cost of the SFO be funded?* An SFO serving the needs of a multi-generational family must consider how costs will be allocated and charged to individual family-member clients of the SFO. Tasks classified as "needs" by a client may slip to the category of "nice to have" when that client finds he must bear the cost.

THE SUCCESSFUL SFO CHECKLIST

What does effectiveness look like in a single family office? How can an SFO achieve exceptional creativity, develop solutions and execute services to meet the family's defined goals? The family (or the SFO leader, if they're so tasked) must consider these questions internally, agree to the answer, and communicate their goals clearly with the CEO of their SFO.

Exceptional SFOs ensure complete alignment and coordination of the family and SFO management and employees, so that they can focus on excellence in achieving the goals the family has identified.

Successful SFOs start at the top with:

- a clear sense of purpose based on the family's vision and goals;
- a dynamic CEO—top HR, recruiters and an organizational psychologist must work together to define the family's objectives and secure the best leader (who may currently not be a CEO or even an SFO executive, but does have a demonstrated track record for achieving outstanding results);
- a top-down management style that is innovative yet disciplined in its approach toward goal-driven outcomes;
- a carefully defined yet flexible culture that is both progressive and inclusive, and adds tremendous value to the family;
- the ability to attract, manage, maximize and retain the right talent to achieve the highest of expectations; and
- an obsession with making the SFO exceptionally effective (reaching desired results), resilient (being able to bounce back from internal and external challenges) and adaptive (able to adjust to constant economic, social, technological and other changes).

The family must agree on and very clearly communicate their goals and the results they expect their SFO leader to achieve in an effective manner. Although defining an

> ## Great Single Family Offices seek employees who are cultural contributors rather than simply a good cultural fit.

effective process is important, strictly following that process should not become more important than achieving the family's ultimate objectives and desired outcomes.

Successful SFO leaders don't follow "group think"—seeking consensus rather than alternative opinions. They encourage debate and dissenting solutions, mutual respect and mindfulness about finding the best answer(s), not simply the best at the moment.

Finding a CEO who embraces these principles is the critical first step in the formula for SFO performance. Once the right leader is secured, the SFO task force should turn its attention to HR.

STRATEGIC HR

Traditionally, HR has been seen as a graveyard for administration and compliance. In today's world, innovative HR is a strategic imperative. We all know that, at the end of the day, the success of the SFO depends on the people it hires. But getting the *right* people on the bus requires that we ask some deeper questions.

First, what does "the right talent" look like?

TRANSFORMING AN SFO

If your SFO isn't starting from scratch, you're reading this book because you don't believe that your SFO has yet achieved world-class performance. The path to success for established SFOs is often more complicated; it will involve bucking the status quo to ask these same questions. Ensuring alignment amongst the family, leadership and talent at the SFO is the only way to be effective.

IN SUMMARY

Designing or restructuring an SFO to fit your family's unique circumstances and needs deserves thought and preparation. Careful planning, alignment of goals/desires, and the selection of the right leader and team members who believe in the principles laid out by the task force—these steps can avert future conflict amongst family office clients, or between the family and the family office.

In the next chapter, we'll see how family governance systems can provide family members with lines of communication and decision-making for defining and managing their expectations.

2

The "G" Word: Creating and Managing Governance

Educated rising family members engaged in the process early, clearly understanding the family origins and legacy, and strong in human capital simply make better decisions.

— JAY HUGHES

Some families shy away from the term "governance." It can bring to mind long lists of onerous rules, regulations and policies. But at its core, governance is nothing to be scared of—it's really nothing more than a set of rules that define how an organization will make decisions, large or small. For governance to be effective, owners, overseers (the board of directors or advisors) and management must be informed; understand their respective roles, rights and responsibilities; and operate the organization accordingly. Once your SFO is established and your leadership team and people are in place, you'll need to turn your attention to either creating or rethinking your governance.

Families of wealth need governance structures—such as a family council, family meetings and boards of directors—that determine who will be included in which decisions. Governance structures may also determine who will work with or at the family office, factoring in how the family wealth is owned (in varying trusts, operational companies and philanthropic foundations).

One of the most common reasons that SFOs fail is that they lack a defined family hierarchy for making decisions and don't have direction and leadership within the SFO. A family with significant first-generation wealth has the clearest path to decision-making. The patriarch and/or matriarch call all the shots.

Legendary investor and founder of Berkshire Hathaway Warren Buffett explains his approach to effective decision-making: "I believe that [the decision-making committee] should be an odd number and less than three." That means one decision-maker: him. While the wealth creator is active, it may make sense for the founder to serve as chairman of the SFO and for the founder and his or her spouse to make the decisions.

As the family expands and rising generations come of age, the founding generation may lose interest, control or, eventually, become disabled and die. This complicates and often compromises decision-making. When the family encompasses many adult beneficiaries, benefactors and rising decision-makers, it's time to establish a three-person family board and choose one of those board members to be the chairman and final decision-maker. It's best to agree to a term limit for the board members and the chairman and to specify those limits in governance documents.

Each person in a large multi-generation family likely brings his or her own desires and conflicts. In-laws can further complicate family decision-making, as they can bring in potentially conflicting family cultures, values and beliefs.

A simple and clear path to decision-making about the direction of the SFO requires creating governance documents that outline guidelines, due process and a means to resolve conflicts. Governance and constitution systems vary from family to family. Some allow family members to elect the board members and the chairman. More consensus-centric families create an odd-numbered board with three or five, allowing majority votes to determine key directional decisions.

Governance has long been a focus of corporate investors, but until recently less attention has been paid to how SFOs are governed. An SFO that intends to serve a family for generations would be wise to encourage the family to develop and implement effective and appropriate family governance structures. Doing so can significantly improve the longevity and success of the office and the family it serves.

The SFO needs to clearly delineate how communication will flow amongst all interested parties.

This should be a collective effort marked by complete transparency and should focus on delivering excellence on the core goals of the SFO.

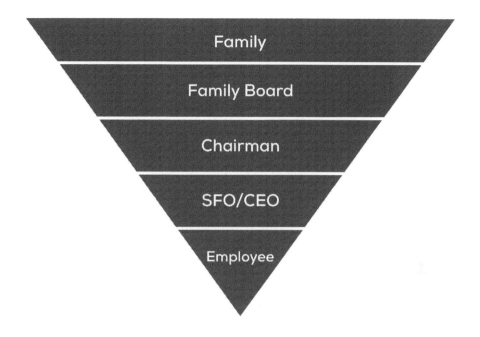

BUILDING IN FLEXIBILITY

One of the challenges of SFO governance is that the needs of the organization may change radically over time—sometimes very suddenly. Governance structures must be robust yet flexible enough to withstand family conflict, generational transitions and cataclysmic changes in the investment environment, whether anticipated or unanticipated.

Commonly, a successful individual will create an SFO following a liquidity event of some sort. The founder will build the SFO structure to suit his own needs and interests. As with any business run by a controlling owner, there isn't a great need for formal governance. At this stage, the owner is fully informed, understands the goals and objectives of the SFO, and handles the critical roles—ownership, stewardship, oversight and management—by themselves. Unless the controlling owner has a formal governance mindset, they generally will prefer to run the SFO "lean and mean," without a lot of staff or formal structure, making decisions on the fly in accordance with their intuitive assessment of what's needed at the moment. The controlling owner will often rely on a key advisor or staff member who knows how to implement the controlling owner's plans, who understands what is needed and does whatever is necessary to make that happen. This sort of organic, first-generation governance generally works quite effectively, at least in the early years. The office runs, makes investments and provides other financial and non-financial services.

However, when the SFO comes to be managed for a wider group—typically, upon the controlling owner's death, when the assets pass to descendants or trusts for their benefit—the absence of established, articulated policies creates a power vacuum. Without the founder around, suddenly no one really knows who's in charge, what needs to be done, who's responsible for doing it, or how that performance will be measured or compensated. If the members of the next generation haven't been prepared for their new roles, there may be a struggle for dominance, or the opposite: fearing conflict, family members may simply abdicate. The SFO may slowly collapse, or a non-family member may come to fill the vacuum, for good or for ill.

TYPES OF FAMILY GOVERNANCE

Here are some of the more common types of governance structures that can help involve, educate and improve communications within wealthy families:

Family Board of Directors. Family participation on the board and in the chairman's role can add value. These individuals should evaluate and vote on the SFO's major strategic direction and policies.

Non-family Family Advisory Board. This entity should be filled with non-family members—often CEOs of more significant businesses in a variety of industries. While advisory board members lack voting rights, they must aim very high and be paid to ensure that the SFO receives the widest possible range of perspectives.

Family Council. Often, a group of family members, representing different branches and generations of the family, meet to discuss issues and concerns that impact the entire family, such as employment of family members, involvement of in-laws, educating the rising generation about family wealth, financial values, and shared vision and mission.

Family Constitution. This is a document that expresses the family's shared legal, financial, emotional and spiritual ideals, values and responsibilities: everything the family deems necessary to create and preserve harmony and health. This document can be drafted by the Family Council members, and then ratified by all adult family members.

Family Meetings. These events provide a time and place for the extended family to share information about the SFO's progress, to educate younger family members about family wealth and values, to discuss family philanthropic direction, and to strengthen family bonds through fun activities.

Family Committees. These involve engaged family members who embrace a deeper purpose than simply being a beneficiary-benefactor. Committees can be formed to focus on human, cultural and social capital. They should be inclusive and transparent. A tax committee, directed by the Chairman and/or CEO, can comprise family members as well as external (to the SFO) tax and legal professionals, who can offer shared ideas and resources to help the SFO achieve the best tax outcome for the family.

KEY ELEMENTS OF EFFECTIVE GOVERNANCE STRUCTURES

Strong governance structures ensure that the SFO operates in accordance with the family's mission and values over multiple generations. The following are key types of governance activities that families can undertake, as needed:

- *The family has articulated its mission, values and vision* for the future, and the strategic plan of the SFO is built around that core. What will be the purpose of this family office? To manage liquidity generated by the sale of a business? To oversee a portfolio of direct investments? To preserve a family legacy? And why does the family want to manage assets collectively? Families planning an SFO should take time at the outset to consider the purpose of the SFO and its role within the family.

  Developing a short, focused mission statement to guide the work of the SFO will help to avoid "mission creep" in future years. The founders should resist drafting a mission statement that is high-minded but vague and short on specifics. A family office consultant can help a family mold its vision and values into a practical and useful tool to guide the work of the SFO.

- *The powers, rights and responsibilities of owners, board and management* are clearly spelled out and followed.

- *The owners have appointed a board of directors and/or advisors* to provide perspective, access to specialized experience/skills, and to discuss strategy and provide guidance. The board includes the family member chairperson, the CEO of the SFO and frequently three others non-conflicted in this capacity (five is commonly an optimum number, three tends to be too clubby).

- *Management is free to implement the SFO's strategy*, without interference or meddling from the family or the owners; although they do need monitoring as to how well they are meeting goals.
- *There are regular owners' and board meetings*, with written agendas and complete minutes. Information necessary for effective decision-making is distributed well in advance of voting, and there is adequate time for discussion.
- *SFO performance reports are clear, comprehensive and timely*, so that decision-making can be based on accurate and complete information.
- *The SFO's strategic plan goes beyond investing* and includes education of family members, for example, to promote effective stewardship over the long-term.

The family does not need to take on all of the above governance activities, but it should focus on those that will best support their needs and goals, and that will most enhance communication, transparency and family cohesion. The chairman must crystalize and clearly communicate to the SFO leader and managers the family's vision, core goals and expected deliverables. These must be held to the highest of standards.

LINES OF AUTHORITY AND ACCOUNTABILITY

The CEO reports to the chairman. Simple. As with a public company, the chairman and the family board are responsible to the family for making sure that the SFO is serving its mission as best as possible.

Aside from accepting direction, guidance and support from the chairman and the board, the CEO should limit distractions. Even from within the family there should be a protocol, in which the CEO submits monthly reports on progress toward goals and an overview of the finances of the SFO, ensuring complete transparency to all family members. There should be at minimum an annual meeting with all family members at which the CEO addresses the family, delivers his or her "state of the union" report, listens to all family members and answers all questions.

While the chairman must be accountable, accountability can have consequences: rifts can occur within the family; disgruntled family members can file lawsuits. It is often a thankless job for the family members in these roles. The more clearly the family can provide the CEO with a clear vision and the governance to achieve it, the better the chance the CEO and the SFO will successfully meet family goals at the highest of standards. Anything else is failure.

The family should create a streamlined process for family members to ask questions of the SFO leader outside of monthly updates and the annual state of the union addresses. A defined process can head off a constant barrage of questions and interruptions that distract the CEO from executing the family's vision and goals. If family members disagree with direction or specific solutions and services, they can reach out to the chairman via a formal process for submitting a grievance, with a timeline for response. Many successful generational families and their SFO CEOs appoint an SFO contact, such as a chief of staff, to field questions and concerns.

Smaller families have a far easier time avoiding divisiveness. In larger families, it sometimes makes sense for dissenting family members to take control over their respective portions of the capital/resources to prevent their conflicting needs from damaging the SFO and allowing it to serve the rest of the family well. Dissenters may find that they can maintain healthy family relationships by breaking off from the SFO.

Whatever governance decisions your SFO makes, making it clear *what* those decisions are is the key to success. Without clear structure and rules, even the best CEO and staff can be gripped by indecision and become ineffective.

Chapter 3 delves into the qualities and experience families should seek when hiring a new CEO of their family office.

3

The Chief Executive Officer

"The first responsibility of a leader is to define reality.
The last is to say thank you. In between, the leader is a servant."

—MAX DE PREE, FORMER CEO OF HERMAN MILLER AND AUTHOR,
"LEADERSHIP IS AN ART" "LEADERSHIP JAZZ" AND "LEADING
WITHOUT POWER"

There is no more critical role in a family office than the Chief Executive Officer. As the preceding chapters have emphasized, it is this man or woman who will bring to life the visions of the family, and either lead the office to success or failure. Finding the right person to fill this role—a person aligned with the family's wishes and able to drive success—can be difficult. To successfully navigate the hiring process, it's important to understand the qualities that make a good leader; and you may find this list of qualities surprising.

In choosing the CEO, many families mistakenly choose a person who is talented in his or her area of expertise, but is not necessarily a true leader and builder of teams. I often see family offices promoting to the executive position Chief Investment Officers or legal and accounting professionals. These individuals, however, tend to see things through their own specialized lens. It is truly worth the effort to find a CEO who possesses the first-rate leadership skills to improve the effectiveness of professionals reporting to him or her, while allowing these professionals to focus on—and enrich the SFO with—their respective areas of expertise. In order to centralize, preserve and transfer significant family wealth across generations and execute the exact services the family wishes, the organizer of an SFO must make the right directional leadership decisions.

THE MAKINGS OF AN EFFECTIVE CEO

CEOs must take responsibility for fulfilling the goals of the family and running an effective organization. Effective CEOs can come from anywhere. Often, families appoint their long-time trusted lawyer or accountant to launch and lead a new SFO. That may work at first, but as the family office assumes responsibility for more and more services, the lawyer or accountant may not possess the newly needed, wider leadership skills and traits such as:

- possessing a track record of achieving great results;
- being the driving force behind success or failure;
- understanding clearly defined goals;
- hiring the right talent; and
- training, overseeing and managing SFO professionals and staff to deliver the family's goals.

"I have not come across a single 'natural,' an executive who was born effective," writes leadership guru Peter Drucker in "The Effective Executive: The Definitive Guide to Getting the Right Things Done" (Harper Business, 2017). "All the effective ones have had to learn to be effective. And all of them then had to practice effectiveness until it became habit. But all the ones who worked on making themselves effective executives succeeded in doing so." Life and business strategist and best-selling author Tony Robbins has said that effective leaders share two other qualities: they think big and have a clearly compelling vision for the future.

Family leaders would be wise to hire an exceptional organizational psychologist, an HR professional and a recruiter to work with the family's chairman and board. Together, they should map out an appropriate CEO profile and coordinate resources to identify and evaluate candidates with the necessary talents, desires and experience.

Candidates should have success in prior leadership positions, even if it wasn't at the CEO level. They should be near the pinnacle of their professions and have experience working with private family businesses. Effective CEOs who are obsessed with success display grace under pressure and practice self-control and extreme discipline when making tough decisions. They are curious and never stop learning or adapting, never getting too comfortable. Even when everything is running smoothly, they always look to improve. They realize if they're not growing and expanding, they cannot provide stability. If they're not improving, the SFO will slowly slip into chaos and failure.

EFFECTIVE DECISION-MAKING

CEOs must tackle problems that may arise every day (many unexpected), possibly delegating to those capable, while staying within the framework of the family's core agreed-to goals.

The late-great Peter Drucker notes that a decision has not truly been made until people know several things:

- the name of the person accountable for carrying it out;
- the deadline;
- the names of people who will be affected by the decision and therefore have to know about, understand, and approve it—or at least not be strongly opposed to it—and;
- the names of the people who have to be informed of the decision even if they are not directly affected by it."

CEOs need to instill in employees a sense of community and teamwork, and communicate that their collective work keeps the family together and helps them thrive. Purpose and mission drive them.

Oversight and accountability are important abilities in a leader. However, the CEO should also practice "eyes-on, hands-off leadership," writes now-retired General Stanley McChrystal in "Team of Teams: New Rules of Engagement for a Complex World" (Portfolio, 2015). The CEO must provide talent with guidance, be approachable to talk with and be a resource, while allowing those they lead the freedom to make decisions. He or she must avoid micro-managing at all costs!

Egos have no place in the SFO, which should be 100 percent dedicated to getting the best answers and solutions to the family's goals. It doesn't matter who provides the best answer or solution. The CEO should constantly seek the best ones, no matter the source. If an SFO's leader is too focused on his or her own glory to do this, the family has the wrong leader.

Dr. Stephen Rudin, founder of Individual U, a leading collaborative mentoring organization, and Matthew Kelly, a scientist, historian, author, and co-principal mentor and Executive Vice President of Individual U, believe that exceptional CEOs constantly develop their skills and possess emotional intelligence, cognitive flexibility and, above all else, complex problem-solving abilities. (Family Office Association, 2016)

BEYOND THE BOX

The popular metaphor "thinking outside the box," is now considered passé. Instead, I believe it's crucial to "think *beyond* the box." We must reach *beyond* our previous mindsets in order to thrive in a world that will soon be defined by new interactions of human, cyber and digital technologies that require *entirely new types of thinking*.

Neurocognitive scientists have been studying the abilities and skills that lead to success in the 21st century. At the top of their list is self-control, particularly the ability to resist the temptation to act impulsively. Discipline and perseverance are required to stay the course and complete tasks. Angela Duckworth, founder of Character Lab writes in her book "Grit: The Power of Passion and Perseverance" (Scribner, 2016), "...no matter what the domain, the highly successful had a kind of ferocious determination that played out in two ways. First, these exemplars were unusually resilient and hardworking. Second, they knew in a very, very deep way what it was they wanted. They not only had determination, they had direction ... In a word, they had grit."

During periods of tremendous change, individuals, small businesses and large businesses must engage in a great deal of trial and error, and resist the temptation to become frustrated. They must persevere, remain focused and avoid distractions from the task at hand. Along the way, profits may fall and confusion may reign. But effective CEOs need the grit to make it through.

A great CEO makes sure people do their jobs with excellence. They never lower the bar. Instead, they challenge and prod employees to achieve their full potential. Bridgewater founder Ray Dalio's "Principles of Success" calls for leaders to "consider daily updates from direct reports as a tool for staying on top of things with your employees. What they are planning to do the next day, their questions, and their observations. "This is similar to the President of the United States receiving daily security and macro updates from his cabinet. But, while I agree with Dalio's suggested daily frequency for newer hires, updates can gradually taper down to weekly as people prove they can deliver desired results.

By finding a CEO who checks all the traditional boxes on leadership *and* has the qualities that will help address emerging concerns in terms of technology, risk and shifting markets, you position your SFO for better adaptability and greater success. Be wary of making internal promotions or hiring family members if they don't meet all the needs. It really is worth it to invest the time in finding the *right* individual to lead your family office.

The next several chapters focus on what it takes to help the family office become more resilient.

4

Ownership of Outcomes

*"Leaders **create** culture, culture shapes behavior
and behavior produces results."*

— TIM KNIGHT, FOUNDER, FOCUS 3

"It is not the strongest of the species that survives, nor the most intelligent, but the one most responsive to change."

— CHARLES DARWIN

"Everyone has a plan until they get hit."

— MIKE TYSON

When committed families create governance that works, hire the right people and manage them to greatness, and then build their SFO from the top down with committed leaders who hold themselves and their staff to high expectations, they have the potential to achieve greatness. However, even many forward-thinking families that do all the right things—including following the suggestions that appear in these chapters—fail to achieve desired results. The same is often true in the corporate world, and even in the military. So what does it take for a family office to be effective and achieve desired outcomes? That's where adaptiveness and resiliency come into play.

LEARNING TO ADAPT

The adaptability of an SFO contributes to long-term, sustained greatness. Changing regulations and tax policies, political upheaval, and evolving family goals over time—all demand that SFO staffers continually adapt the way they provide services. No matter how strong or innovative an SFO may be, the CEO needs to make sure it can adapt to a constantly changing environment.

"[E]very success creates new opportunities," writes Peter Drucker in "The Effective Executive." He continues, "So does every failure. The same is true for changes in the business environment, in the market, and especially in people within the enterprise—all these changes demand that the plan be revised. A written plan should anticipate the need for flexibility."

Kevin Kelly, author of "The Inevitable: Understanding the 12 Technological Forces That Will Shape Our Future" (Viking, 2016), believes that "everything is mutable to customer usage, feedback, competition, innovation, and wear." Even valued creations must transform over time. CEOs must manage change to continue improving. If they don't, the SFO's performance will slip; however, while operating practices and business strategies are subject to change, what the family and its SFO stand for and why they exist should not. A CEO must understand and negotiate that difference.

The CEO must seek to maintain excellence, not just to avoid mistakes. This must resonate from the top down. Structures, resources and expert employees alone are not sufficient. The very best global businesses and organizations have been dedicated to these principles for years. Researchers, authors and consultants such as Peter Drucker, Jim Collins, Adam Grant and Steven Covey have described and analyzed strategies and tactics of renowned leaders. Corporate leaders such as Ray Dalio, Jack Welch, Warren Buffett, Jack Ma, Indra Nooyi, Bill Belichick and others have executed these principles exceptionally well.

McChrystal learned that the key to achieving and sustaining success requires more than doing all the right things. When he took command in 2003 of the U.S. Joint Special Operations Command (JSOC)—an umbrella team of the Navy SEALS, Army Rangers and Delta Force—his mission was to beat al-Qaida in Iraq. Part of the Stanford Graduate School of Business "View From The Top" speaker series, McChrystal explained in a 2014 presentation, "I expected that if we got better and better at what we did, if we honed what we did, shoot straighter, fly faster ... then our technological and quality mismatch would allow us to win." [1]

But, while successful at the tactical level, McChrystal's team was not winning the war. "We eventually figured out that it was necessary, but not sufficient, to have the best people, the most advanced technology, training and strategy." The missing ingredient was adaptability, which McChrystal defines as "the difference between doing things right—doing by established processes, habit, training—and doing things the right way ... [W]e carried the baggage of doing things right ... against an enemy whose only metric was survival. So efficiency comes up against adaptability, and efficiency comes out the loser ... We tried to take the best of what we do, put it together with extreme adaptability, changed the way we thought and operated, to make it work."

The result was an increased sense of trust and purpose throughout the team. Gen. McChrystal created what he calls an "emotional linkage" and a "contextual linkage" (shared information), to create a "shared consciousness." He learned that "efficiency or effectiveness of the team ... is a function of the individual excellence, talent, commitment of individuals and shared consciousness ... that almost-magic elixir that changes that relationship."

SEPARATING BUSINESS FROM FAMILY

Why do so many of the world's most successful families rarely apply such successful principles and philosophies to their SFO? One huge reason is that families often consider their SFO almost an extension of the family, not a business. Families expect their SFO to provide the ultimate in service, and to preserve and transfer significant family wealth across generations. It makes no sense that family leaders' commitment to their SFO's greatness is often little more than an afterthought. Like any companies that have sustained success, SFOs need aspirational leadership, professionalism and rigorous processes aligned to the highest expectations.

Paul Morelli, founder of Vernal Advisors, points out, "Truth is, many families simply can't mount the effort it takes to create a great single family office. Either they have to lead, or to recruit and retain a great leader, and to do this they have to actually think empathetically about their professionals' goals and aspirations. But the reality is that

---

1 https://www.gsb.stanford.edu/insights/gen-stanley-mcchrystal-adapt-win-21st-century

most families think it's all about themselves, which leads to a huge drop in interest and motivation in the professional ranks for those types of professionals considering to join an SFO."

In "Tools of Titans: The Tactics, Routines, and Habits of Billionaires, Icons, and World-Class Performers" (Houghton Mifflin Harcourt, 2016), author Tim Ferriss reveals another reason SFOs frequently fail to follow successful principles when he quotes Marc Andreessen, co-founding partner of Andreessen & Horowitz: "Every billionaire suffers from the same problem. Nobody around them says, 'Hey, that idea you just had is really stupid.'"

Maintaining a healthy separation between family and the business of the SFO, and encouraging questions and debate are keys to achieving desired outcomes.

EMBRACING DISRUPTION

Considering that every entrepreneur, every business, every company will at some point be disrupted, many smart CEOs in the corporate world and at SFOs practice disrupting themselves to avoid complacency and to remain flexible and spry.

In "Tools of Titans," Ferriss quotes Peter Diamandis, founder and executive chairman of the XPRIZE Foundation, who was named one of the World's 50 Greatest Leaders by *Fortune* magazine: "One of the most fundamental realizations is that every entrepreneur, every business, every company will get disrupted. I've had the honor of talking with Jeff Immelt, the CEO of GE, in his leadership team meetings. The same thing for Muhtar Kent, chairman and CEO of Coca-Cola, and for Cisco and for many companies. I ask them, 'How will you disrupt yourself, and how are you trying to disrupt yourself? If you're not, you're in for a real surprise.' Find the smartest 20-somethings in your company. I don't care if they're in the mailroom or where they are. Give them permission to figure out how they would take down your company."

While strategy is very important, an SFO needs a plan that can help it not only achieve its strategic goals, but also be flexible in order to react to disruption with strategic split-second decisions. SFOs must lead and teach employees to expect disruption and adapt to meet challenges, and remain creative yet disciplined.

ASKING QUESTIONS

Truly enlightened leaders follow many of the principles that revolutionary finance legend and hedge fund manager Ray Dalio, founder of Bridgewater Associates, follows and recommends. For instance, Dalio points out that exceptional leaders stress-test ideas by having the smartest people they know challenge them. For the greatest benefit, such leaders focus not just on their conclusions, but also on the reasoning that led them to their conclusions.

CEOs and family leaders can improve and sustain superlative outcomes by brainstorming answers to basic questions. In "Five Most Important Questions: Enduring Wisdom for Today's Leaders" (Jossey-Bass, 2015), authors Peter Drucker, Frances Hesselbein and Joan Snyder Kuhl point out the most important questions for any business, including:

- Who is our customer?
- What does the customer value?
- What are our results?
- What is our plan?

This may sound easy, especially for an SFO serving one family. But many SFO leaders have a tough time answering these questions. Organizations (be they small or large, educational institutions or government agencies) can start by considering significant new or potential external or internal challenges, opportunities and issues.

A wise SFO leader also encourages employees to ask probing questions during regular meetings with direct reports, and as applicable, meetings of the full staff. Doing so enhances alignment and commitment to the SFO's goals, illustrates progress and provides an opportunity to discuss challenges in an open community. It also helps democratize accountability for progress and showcases to everyone how the SFO needs to proceed. These are appropriate times to debate the merit of a given approach and to encourage open dissent about direction and methods for achieving specific goals. Minutes from these meetings should be recorded and transcribed not just to clarify who's responsible for next steps, but to help train new employees.

The CEO should consider setting up committees, such as tax, IT and investments. Professionals from inside and outside the SFO who are smart, talented and opinionated should serve on these committees. Their mission is not to seek consensus, but to discover the best answers and solutions. Outside sources (which, pending chairman approval, may need to be compensated) bring new eyes to the challenges and opportunities.

The CEO must engage and manage the right employees in a very transparent manner. It's impossible to overstate the importance of debating ideas and challenging the status quo in an open environment. Criticism should be welcome, even encouraged. As Dalio points out, being curious and open-minded is far more important than being smart. He recommends that CEOs:

- Embrace conflicts as a great way to resolve differences and align company principles;
- Hold employees accountable for outcomes while giving them the authority to achieve desired outcomes;
- Appreciate them holding YOU accountable. Nothing is more valuable to personal growth than accurate criticisms;
- Hire people who ask great questions;
- Do *not* lower the bar. Challenge and probe employees to achieve their potential; and
- Utilize daily updates from direct reports as a tool for staying on top of what employees are planning to do the next day, their questions and their observations.

Achieving adaptability requires honesty and transparency. Deal with realities head on. Be truthful about your mistakes and weaknesses. Truth, the accurate understanding of reality, is essential for producing good outcomes. Everything from governance structure and culture to leadership and talent should be geared toward creating an adaptive, agile company that can reach success.

5

Maintaining a Learning Mindset

"The definition of vision must be rooted in providing answers to probing questions such as, 'What is our business? What will it be? What should it be?'"

— PETER DRUCKER

It's up to the chairman of the family board (or perhaps the consensus of a three-person or five-person board) to set the vision and goals for SFO direction and hire a CEO who can provide top-down leadership to execute those goals. But that's only the first step in ensuring that the leadership of your family office is in place. Once you find the right person to fill the role of CEO, it's important to give them the resources to maintain a learning mindset within the organization—and help them spread this culture to the staff.

PERPETUAL LEARNING
If the CEO lacks a "beginner's mind"—a willingness to consider many ideas, unrestricted by the preconceived notions of an expert—his or her staff will likely follow suit. Openness to continual learning must start at the top. The good news is that the attitudes and attributes of great leaders can be acquired. After interviewing many great leaders, the late organizational consultant and pioneer in leadership studies Warren Bennis found, "They all agreed leaders are made, not born, and made more by themselves than by any external means." Bennis concluded, "Everyone, of whatever age and circumstance, is capable of self-transformation."

A culture built around perpetual learning must not just focus on advances in the services employees perform for the family, but about the family itself. The SFO must recognize that families change and evolve, and that their multi-generational nature requires them to construct interactions differently as time goes on. As families change and evolve, so must the SFO. The family office must remain "tuned in" to the family dynamics that influence the conversations and interactions occurring between family members, between the family and the SFO, and between the family and the social community at-large.

How can the CEO foster constant training and learning for themselves as well as everyone in the organization? Classes, in-house instructors, organizational psychologists and HR professionals can be extremely helpful when it comes to testing prospects and existing employees to identify this mindset of perpetual learning.

"Work how you work best (and let others do the same)," recommends Jim Collins, in the foreword to the latest edition of Peter Drucker's classic "The Effective Executive."

"Some people work well at night; others work better in the morning. Some absorb information best by reading, others by listening. Some thrive in full immersion; others work better in short bursts with variety in the day. Some are project oriented; others are process oriented ... [W]e are wired for ways of working in the same way we are right-handed or left-handed ... No one but you can take responsibility to leverage how you best work, and the sooner you do, the more years you have to gain the cumulative effect of tens of thousands of hours well spent."

DOUBLE VISION

We covered the importance of defining the family's vision and goals in the chapter on governance. It's also critical to understand this must be treated as a continual process of defining and aligning. The family and its SFO must work in concert to identify each entity's (the family's and SFO's) vision. They may be quite different. For instance, the family may decide its vision is to help all members lead healthy, fulfilling and well-balanced lives. The SFO's vision may be to help its staff acquire the resources, training, values and incentives to help the family achieve its vision.

The following strategic questions can help the family and its SFO leader determine how the family office will operate to meet the family's needs and expectations:

- Have you clarified the SFO's vision—why the SFO exists?
- What are the key priorities for achieving the vision—its mission?
- Are family members, board members, SFO executives and employees clearly aware of the vision, and are they reminded of it constantly (via the SFO's culture)?
- Are everything and everyone in the SFO aligned with achieving the vision (via training)?
- Does the SFO leader spend significant time on the SFO's key goals and priorities?

Let's look at each of these elements:

Vision defines what a family or organization wants to become. Warren Bennis, organizational consultant and author, has said that leaders must have "an overreaching vision, to set an example of passion, curiosity, integrity and daring for the others in the organization." The vision should encompass the primary benefits the family expects to derive from its SFO.

TOP-DOWN LEADERSHIP

VISION	Who are we and what does the family want?
MISSION	What is the best strategy for fulfilling the family's vision?
CULTURE	What environment, attitudes and practices will enable the SFO to implement the family's strategic plan?
RESOURCES	Are there ample resources to accomplish the goals, including technology and information?
TRAINING	Is training ongoing with an eye toward improving everyone's adaptability to a constantly changing reality?
SPECTACULAR RESULTS	

A world-class SFO must limit its scope to defining what the family values the most. The SFO should not do anything else. As the great author Jim Collins has written, the "not-to-do list" is as important as the "to-do list" The SFO should only perform services that are most important to the family and become great at those things. Other services should be outsourced to other excellent organizations.

No matter how inspired and relevant the vision, the SFO (and the family) will be doomed to mediocrity unless the SFO leader translates that vision into a strategic mission.

Mission seeks to answer the question, "What are we here to do?" by looking at the business from the outside, from the point of view of the customer. (In an SFO, that's the family). According to Drucker, "To satisfy the customer is the mission and purpose of every business." SFO management must accept what the family sees, thinks, believes and wants at any given time. Like all customers, family members want to know what the product or service will do for them tomorrow. A well-crafted mission includes policies and benchmarks that keep everyone on track to achieve the vision.

The SFO's culture must create an environment that welcomes and rewards open and constructive communication, enables teamwork, and celebrates each employee's personal development and contributions to the organization's and the family's success. Max Dupree, in his book "Leadership is an Art" (Doubleday, 2004), writes that the function of the leader is "to give others the space to be what they can be." If employees approach their individual potential, so will the organization.

Ample resources include talent, technology, information and money.

Training should focus on keeping staff up-to-date in their functional areas (such as accounting, investing, legal, taxes, cyber and physical security, etc.), as well as honing their communication and people skills. Training should be ongoing, with an eye toward improving everyone's ability to adapt to a constantly changing reality.

Spectacular results stem from SFO leaders who lavish attention on vision, mission, culture, resources and training.

CONSTANT QUESTIONS

Barbara Minto, who began her career at McKinsey and then formed her own trade-marked principles (the Minto Pyramid Principle and Minto Books International), believes that effective leaders and employees must always be asking questions:

WHAT SHOULD WE DO?

- How should we do it?
- Should we do it?
- Why did it happen?

IS THERE A PROBLEM?

- Where does it lie?
- Why does it exist?
- What could we do about it?
- What should we do about?

IS THERE AN OPPORTUNITY?

- Where does it lie?
- Why does it exist?
- What could we do about it?
- What should we do about?

Next, Chapter 6 delves into the attributes SFOs should look for when hiring, evaluating and training employees.

6

Filling the Bus

*"People are not the most important asset; the **right** people are."*

— JIM COLLINS, AUTHOR OF *GOOD TO GREAT* AND *BUILT TO LAST*

Once structure, leadership and culture are in place, it's time to fill the bus. Just like the CEO position, it's important to realize that the most talented specialist may not always be the right person for other positions in an SFO. Indeed, each employee at the family office must embrace the vision and culture that have been established. The best candidates will be willing to learn, be resourceful and innovative, and demonstrate humility in service and discretion. Along with these skills, it's also crucial to screen for impeccable character and ethics, dedication, pride in commitment and, dare I say, honor. These can ensure that the SFO gets the *right* people—as Collins tell us is critical—on the bus, and the wrong people off the bus.

In this chapter, you'll find several often-overlooked hiring criteria, recommendations for developing dynamic diversity in the SFO, and ways to assess employees that new leadership might inherit from previous leaders. There are of course the standard criteria that you should use to evaluate an employee—personality, past performance, skills—but here are some skills you may not have previously considered that can prove to be even more important.

A very successful colleague of mine is known to say that he would rather hire a janitor who is an "A player" and train him than hire a "C player" who already has the requisite skills. Time and again, we find this to be true—hiring top-notch people using the criteria below is the key to creating a well-tuned, effective family office.

OFTEN OVERLOOKED HIRING CRITERIA

There are several important traits to seek when hiring new or assessing inherited employees. I like to recommend that family offices begin the evaluation process by determining whether a candidate is a "giver" or a "taker."

Givers vs. Takers. After 9/11, Harvard psychologists worked with the U.S. Intelligence system to determine what makes intelligence units effective.[2] Adam Grant, author of "Give and Take: A Revolutionary Approach to Success" (Viking, April 2013), describes the researchers' finding that the critical factor wasn't stable team membership or the right number of people. It wasn't having a vision that is clear, challenging and meaningful. Nor was it well-defined roles and responsibilities' appropriate rewards, recognition, and resources; or strong leadership. All those factors are important, of course. But the strongest predictor of group effectiveness was the amount of help that analysts gave to each other. The highest-performing analyst teams invested extensive time and energy in coaching, teaching and consulting with their colleagues.

In "giver cultures," employees operate as high-performing intelligence units do: sharing knowledge, offering mentoring and making connections without expecting anything in return. In "taker cultures," the norm is to get as much as possible from others while contributing less in return.

Grant's research suggests that committed leaders can encourage a "giver culture" with three practices:

- facilitating help-seeking;
- recognizing and rewarding givers; and
- screening out takers.

What techniques help identify a taker personality? Grant points to three reliable ways to distinguish takers from others. Takers tend to:

---

2 McKinsey Insights' interview with Adam Grant appears at http://www.mckinsey.com/business-functions/organization/our-insights/givers-take-all-the-hidden-dimension-of-corporate-culture (accessed December 9, 2016)

- claim personal credit for successes;
- follow a pattern of "kissing up, kicking down"; and
- sometimes engage in antagonistic behavior at the expense of others.

With this logic in mind, Georgia Tech professor Larry James led a pioneering series of studies validating an assessment called the Conditional Reasoning Test for Aggression. The test is designed to unveil antagonistic tendencies with a cleverly designed questionnaire featuring reasoning problems that lack obvious answers. By screening out candidates with antagonistic tendencies, leaders can increase the odds of selecting applicants who will behave as givers.

The knowledge-sharing that takes place in giver cultures is extremely valuable. Sharing great ideas within the SFO and between SFO leaders does not water them down; it creates opportunities for others to build on and transform ideas into strategies and tactics that benefit everyone involved.

Managers vs. makers. Some people and roles require more creativity than others. Paul Graham, founder of Y Combinator, points out that *managers* like organization and structure, keep their calendar full with meetings and measure progress through activity and quantifiable successes. *Makers* are more creative. They need to focus, often for long periods, on a specific task and work best with no distractions, and on their own time frame.[3] Both managers and makers can have a place in your family office, but it's important to understand which category a potential hire falls into when deciding whether they're right for the role you need to fill. And understanding the way each employee best works will also help your team increase productivity and become more effective.

Gumption is another soft, but important, trait that many hirers fail to consider. No matter an employee's position, it's important that they have the gumption to challenge the status quo and take initiative; and they should granted the freedom within their positional framework to create the job they want. Organizations benefit when employees feel ownership of their roles, yet are encouraged to freely contribute their knowledge and skills to others in the organization.

---

3 For more information about managers versus makers, see http://paulgraham.com/makersschedule.html

CREATING A TALENT PIPELINE

So how do you find top talent to begin with? In "Who: The A Method for Hiring" (Ballantine Books, 2008), authors Geoff Smart and Randy Street describe the approach of Patrick Ryan, founder of Aon Corporation: "Whenever he meets somebody new, he asks this simple, powerful question: 'Who are the most talented people you know that I should hire?' Talented people know talented people, and they're almost always glad to pass along one another's names. Ryan captures those names on a list, and he makes a point of calling a few new people from his list every week. Then he stays in touch with those who seem to have the most promise."

Smart and Street recommend tapping your professional and personal networks for superior referrals. Commit to calling one of the ten most talented people you know each week for the next ten weeks to ask, "Who are the most talented people you know?"

Employees are another great source of potential new talent. Smart and Street recommend including sourcing as an outcome on each team member's scorecard[4]—for example, sourcing five "A" players each year who pass the organization's phone screen and offering a referral bonus. Encourage employees to ask people in their networks, "Who are the most talented people you know that I should recommend?" A referral bounty can motivate select friends of the firm (including clients, advisors, vendors) to recommend talent. The bounty could be a small gift certificate or a significant cash bonus.

When using recruiters, provide them with a scorecard to specify your requirements. Also make sure hiring researchers understand your business and culture.

Create a sourcing system (such as a candidate-tracking system integrated with your calendar) that captures the names and contact information on everybody you source, Smart and Street recommend, and schedule weekly time to follow up.

By following this approach you're sure to locate true "A" players. Teaching new skills to an A player is much easier in the long run than trying to turn a C player into an A player, regardless of the skills they start off with.

---

4 The authors suggest creating a scorecard for each employee, defining a set of outcomes and competencies that create a job well done.

DYNAMIC DIVERSITY OF EMPLOYEES

Diversity in the workplace is important not only to comply with the law, it also makes good business sense. Studies consistently show that more diverse workplaces post better financial performances. "Companies in the top quartile for racial and ethnic diversity are 35 percent more likely to have financial returns above their respective national industry medians," and gender diverse firms see 15 percent higher results.[5] These are numbers that family offices cannot continue to ignore.

Hiring a blend of people of different ages, cultures, faiths, and genders will help your talent work in adaptive and creative ways. For instance, older employees may find it difficult to keep up with the latest technology, while younger people are often native to high tech, artificial intelligence and virtual reality—all of which are playing an increasingly important role in the SFO world, as well as the broader business and financial worlds. Older workers often have a richer wealth of experience that younger employees may lack. Why choose? You can benefit by maintaining a blend of older and younger employees on your staff.

Your HR staff and an organizational psychologist can coordinate to determine the traits to seek from a diverse group of employees who will add value to the culture—with an eye toward hiring more women and people of color, and a blend of youthful and older, more experienced employees.

For instance, you might seek candidates who:

- are givers;
- have character;
- are courageous, curious, resourceful and open-minded;
- practice self-control;
- are creative yet disciplined;
- possess empathy and humility, as well as grit.

DEFINING ROLES

After finding employees with the right cultural fit and mindset, it's important to give them the resources to be successful in their roles. The first step to being successful

---

5 http://www.mckinsey.com/business-functions/organization/our-insights/why-diversity-matters

is defining what success looks like. We've already done this at the family office level, but it's just as important to do this at the employee level, providing each individual a description of what it means to succeed in his or her role.

Authors Smart and Street suggest one to five sentences describing why each role exists. For instance, "The mission for the customer service representative is to help customers resolve their questions and complaints with the highest level of courtesy possible." They also recommend developing three to eight specific, objective outcomes that each employee must accomplish to achieve an "A" performance. Make those outcomes quantitative and provide deadlines whenever possible. For example, "Improve family satisfaction on a ten-point scale from 7.1 to 9.0 by Dec. 31."

Also, identify role-based competencies to describe behaviors you expect from employees to achieve desired outcomes, along with five to eight competencies that describe the SFO's culture. Place the mission, objective outcomes, role-based and cultural competencies on the scorecard for every position. For example, "Competencies include efficiency, honesty, high standards, and a customer service mentality."

Lastly, Smart and Street advocate pressure-testing each scorecard by comparing it with the business plan and scorecards of employees who will interact with the person in the role, to ensure consistency and alignment. Then share the scorecard with relevant parties, including peers and recruiters.

UNDERSTANDING YOUR EMPLOYEE NEEDS

Depending on the mission of the SFO, it will hire staff in a variety of areas:

Legal professionals can help SFOs preserve and transfer family resources, often through a complex series of trusts and corporate entities. In addition, the changing political, regulatory, tax and family landscape requires frequent analysis and proactive adjustment. An attorney experienced and trusted in business-investment matters can also be a great internal resource for families that actively invest in real estate and/or are direct investors.

Tax experts historically are an integral part of any SFO. They should coordinate with the internal legal professionals in their efforts to preserve and transfer family resources; they should also coordinate with internal investment professionals. This allows the greatest synchronization of tax arbitrage and other advancing planning strategies. Progressive tax planning can be the most valuable direct monetary benefit any SFO may deliver to the family.

These services are so important that the SFO and family should form a tax committee, composed of the chairman, CEO, other internal SFO tax resources and various outside representative organizations used by the family or SFO in managing taxes. Few SFOs create a tax committee, but it's all but impossible for an SFO to be effective and tax-proactive without one.

Chief Investment Officers (CIOs) focus on investment policy, asset allocation and execution of the investment strategy—whether direct, outsourced through third party managers, or (commonly) a combination. CIOs commonly need supporting resources such as analyst(s).

Human Resources specialists (in larger SFOs), internal or external, serve as an exceptional trusted resource to the family and the SFO leadership. This function involves as much art as science when sourcing and selecting the right people for the team. HR specialists test employees and potential hires for good alignment with—and ability to add value to—the company culture; they also design measurable metrics for goals-driven achievement.

An executive assistant to the CEO will manage his or her schedule and commitments, and proactively serve as a liaison between the CEO and the family. The executive assistant should attempt to address family members' questions by tapping the SFO's experts and resources. Large SFOs may even hire a chief of staff—a family liaison professional with exceptional organizational and people skills who helps family members with SFO services and sourcing from within the SFO.

Supporting services can include secretarial services, assistants/associates to the positions already described, and the use of interns for various research and other projects.

Interns can round out an SFO's staff by assisting the current talent in the SFO. One-year programs look better on an intern's resume (leaving after a year is expected of interns) and the cost is relatively low for the SFO: $40,000 to $75,000 per year. A family office can hire interns to help develop technology and apps, conduct research or arrange logistics for family meetings. A high-quality intern may even be able to look at everything the SFO does and question it totally, providing a stress-test of the

SFO's current ways of operating and opening the SFO to improvement from a young, creative mind.

When hiring interns, SFOs should source graduates of top-level business schools such as Stanford or Columbia by posting on university job boards and attending job fairs at the universities. This provides opportunities for families and SFO leaders to be exposed to top minds and creative business thinkers, especially if a CEO is in place and their role includes sourcing and training talent.

SFOs may not be able to attract A-plus Stanford computer science engineers, but they can attract those who are a notch just below that. It's important to make the SFO sound attractive. Working for an incredibly successful family and the private company that manages their resources does sound somewhat exciting. Another plus is the opportunity to gain exposure to the family and SFO's network of top professionals and expert advisors.

Screening interns is an opportunity for executives to illustrate to the CEO their ability to choose well and train staff. In American football parlance, this is known as "coaching up." Some intern positions can be a testing ground for potential full-time, permanent talent.

ASSESSING INHERITED EMPLOYEES

If you aren't starting a family office from scratch, there are other considerations to keep in mind—particularly, the existing staff and how they fit into the newly transformed governance, leadership and culture. Newly hired leaders need to tread somewhat carefully, taking plenty of time to evaluate existing talent and provide guidance. As long as the CEO has family buy-in, he or she should evaluate inherited employees to learn who seems to grasp and embrace the new leader's direction and vision, and who are givers or takers.

In "The Effective Executive," Peter Drucker insists, "An organization needs to bring in fresh people with fresh points of view fairly often. If it only promotes from within it soon becomes inbred and eventually sterile. But if at all possible, one does not bring in the newcomers where the risk is exorbitant—that is, into the top executive positions or into leadership of an important new activity. One brings them in just below the top and into an activity that is already defined and reasonably well understood."

While letting some workers go may erode morale at first, the keepers will sense that the new CEO has been thoughtful and fair and has given everyone a chance. For instance, the new CEO can set up a trial period to gauge which employees are most capable of helping move the SFO forward. While communicating very clearly the SFO's goals and expectations, it's important not to lower the standards. The CEO must provide the support, resources and training employees need to succeed, assuming they are technically capable and ethical, possess character and grit, and are driven to excellence.

When the CEO identifies areas in which some inherited employees may need to change their behaviors, the process begins with leadership and clear cultural focus. In this circumstance, the new leader needs to manage top-down to help the talent progress and to build mutual trust. As trust is earned, the CEO can give employees more latitude in proactive decision-making and using creativity to achieve excellence on their stated goals. Daily reports and clear communication between the CEO and those reporting to him or her are crucial. In other words, the CEO needs to get out of the ivory tower and into the trenches, and be willing get their hands dirty.

Ideally, this requires the CEO to not necessarily tell staff (inherited or not) what to do, but to provide feedback and allow debate before employees move forward with and execute new ideas, plans and processes.

In "Turn the Ship Around: The True Story of Turning Followers into Leaders" (Portfolio, 20013), author L. David Marquet suggests that CEOs should ask inherited employees:

- "What are the things you're hoping I don't change?"
- "What are things you hope I secretly do change?"
- "If you were me what would you do first?"
- "Why isn't the SFO doing better?"
- "What are important professional/personal goals for you?"
- "What impediments do you face in doing your job?"
- "What will be my biggest challenges?"

When a new leader begins making changes, especially with staff, it often feels threatening to existing employees. It's possible to preserve morale by making sure the evaluation process is fair and gives all employees a chance.

MOTIVATING EMPLOYEES

Many families and SFO leaders focus almost exclusively on financial incentives to motivate employees. This is a huge mistake. Non-monetary rewards can be quite effective for enhancing the performance of individuals and teams.

- *Intrinsic Rewards.* "The performance of the task provides intrinsic reward," notes Daniel H. Pink in his book "Drive: The Surprising Truth About What Motivates Us" (the LatestEdition, 2009). "Things like enjoyment of the work itself, genuine achievement, and personal growth. These internal desires were what really boosted both satisfaction and performance and were where managers ought to focus their attention," Pink writes.

  Edward L. Deci, professor of psychology and Gowen Professor in the Social Sciences at the University of Rochester adds, "One who is interested in developing and enhancing intrinsic motivation in children, employees, students, etc., should not concentrate on external-control systems such as monetary rewards."

  "Mastery is a mindset," according to Stanford University psychology professor Carol Dweck, who has been studying motivation and achievement in children and young adults for almost four decades. Dweck has found that what people achieve is shaped by what they believe, including what they believe about themselves and their abilities. What she calls our "self-theories" determine how we interpret our experiences and how we set boundaries around what we accomplish.

  "One source of frustration in the workplace is the frequent mismatch between what people must do and what people can do. When what they must do exceeds their capabilities, the result is anxiety. When what they must do falls short of their capabilities, the result is boredom. But when the match is just right, the results can be glorious. This is the essence of flow."

- *Extrinsic rewards* "should be unexpected and offered only after the task is complete," writes Pink.

  "Praise and positive feedback are much less corrosive than cash and trophies," writes Deci. In his original experiments, and in his subsequent analysis of other studies, Deci found that "positive feedback can have an enhancing effect on intrinsic motivation." He recommends regularly walking into each team's office and praising their recent efforts or accomplishments. "It sounds small and simple," Deci says, "but it can have an enormous effect."

Pink adds, "In the workplace, people are thirsting to learn about how they're doing, but only if the information isn't a tacit effort to manipulate their behavior. So don't tell the design team: 'That poster was perfect. You did it exactly the way I asked.'" Instead, he suggests giving team members specific feedback focusing on effort and strategy rather than outcome.

- *Informational motivators.* Pink points out that there are three pinnacles of success: autonomy, mastery and purpose. "Autonomous people working toward mastery perform at very high levels. But those who do so in the service of some greater objective can achieve even more."

In business, leaders focus on telling employees *how* to perform tasks, but rarely spend time on the "why." According to Pink, "A powerful way to provide that context is to spend a little less time telling how and a little more time showing why."

- *Financial Rewards.* It's best for the family to provide top-percentile base compensation and core traditional benefits to SFO talent. Bonuses based on outcomes often become expected entitlements, which over time can erode performance. Monetary rewards tied to specific non-team tasks decrease commitment to the team, do not reward "givers," and often backfire in the long-term. This is not to say that there should be no end-of-year team-centric bonus compensation.

The SFO should provide a pathway for executive and employee career development. That may make your talent attractive to other organizations, but it's better to have that problem than underperforming talent. The trick is to ensure that employees strive to achieve ambitious success for the SFO, rather than focusing on maximizing their own financial rewards. Of course, they need to be compensated well and treated as an important part of the team.

SFO leaders must provide leadership, support and training to all employees, and exceptional hands-on coaching to direct reports; however, if they need to spend time motivating executives and employees to diligently perform their duties and fulfill the organization's mission, then the SFO has the wrong people on staff. Game over.

Whom you pay is more important than how you pay them. Families and SFO leaders need to be sympathetic to the goals and aspirations of their employees. In order to attract great people who can build a great SFO, the SFO must offer competitive salaries and benefits. In addition to a competitive salary and core employee benefits (health, life and disability insurance; vacation time; etc.), ancillary benefits in particular—in competitive environments and markets—will help attract and retain the right talent. Such benefits could include a pet-friendly work environment, catered high-quality food, dry cleaning services, time off for volunteering, games rooms, etc.

A team-focused bonus plan can still be a valuable compensation strategy for some SFOs. Wall Street firms, global consultancies, top legal and accounting firms, and many other competitive industries follow a team-oriented, holistic approach in which a discretionary bonus depends on the success of the unit and the organization as a whole. A professional compensation organization experienced in serving SFOs can help define the metrics for success and compensation, along with other best practices. It is usually best is to overpay on core compensation for the right people and pay less for individual bonus based performance.

Family members who work in the SFO should be fairly compensated just as any other employee. Some families and SFO leaders assume that as a beneficiary of the trusts and services, family member employees should work as a service to the family. But if they are qualified enough to get hired, they should be paid appropriately.

Family Office Association's comprehensive Single Family Office Best Practices Checklist provides a framework for items to review annually in the SFO.

Leading progressive SFOs also offer their investment professionals—more commonly in direct-investing SFOs—a percentage of the profits (above a certain benchmark). Incentive alignment for families should not be built on overly aggressive investment risk. The family is more likely in the stay-rich business than the get-richer business.

Sometimes, instead of being directly part of the SFO, direct-investing professionals and their team work best as separate entities—as an investment management company that is provided different metrics, compensation, leadership direction and reporting to the family. This requires them to work internally and exclusively with the family. They'll likely need a big upside tied to the long-term investment success with a piece of the action. The family provides the money and perhaps leadership, back-office services and support, perhaps connections and compensation incentives. Golden handcuffs can be useful to assure long-term alignment.

No matter the method of engagement, the family needs to have in place proper legal arrangements such as employee agreements, employee code of conduct guidelines, employee manuals, non-disclosure agreements, privacy statements and other documents deemed applicable by the family's legal counsel.[6]

CREATING CULTURE-BASED INCENTIVES FOR TOP TALENT

Great companies such as Google and Facebook attract, retain and incentivize the top talent in their fields by offering not just high pay and benefits, but also a work environment in which employees can flourish because they have opportunities to learn and grow in their positions, making them feel enthused, respected and listened to. Some companies are so good at creating these deep incentives that top talent is willing to trade more lucrative salaries from other employers to join their teams. Amazon is notorious for having some of the most talent people across a variety of sectors, and yet the highest salary at the company (Bezos included) is only $160,000. Employees who could easily fetch sums much higher than this are instead incentivized with stock options, autonomy and other perks that make them devoted, life-long evangelists.

SFOs with the right leadership and direction can emulate some of these companies' techniques for making the workplace irresistibly attractive:

- *Create radical transparency.* Everyone knows their role and how much everyone is compensated. When employees are afraid that others know their compensation, it's because they think they are not worthy.
- *Form a bonus pool* that is based on clear metrics and is shared equally by all, from the highest to the lowest salaried employee. If the SFO with nine employees sets aside $1.5 million for bonuses, each person would receive $166,667.

---

6 Valve Software has published its excellent, must-read employee manual online: http://www.valvesoftware.com/company/Valve_Handbook_LowRes.pdf.

- *Design an open-architecture office environment* with no fancy corner offices: this is open and team friendly. The use of natural light, glass and fun, lively patterns makes coming to work like hanging out in your living room—it just feels comfortable to be there.
- *Allow employees to set their own hours* as long as they are effective at their jobs.
- *Allow all employees to grade their superiors.*
- *Offer treadmill desks for the health conscious.*
- *Consider being a dog-friendly office.*
- *Consider other perks like dry-cleaning, free meals, no dress code.*

Relaxing the traditional workplace environment and providing more attractive and tangible incentives can help attract younger talent.

OUTSOURCING SERVICES

SFOs often outsource to providers, vendors and services when they lack internal talent and experience, or when outsiders can be less expensive than in-house professionals. When outsourcing, it's important that external providers be best-in-class. SFOs must demand transparency so they can fully understand the costs and benefits of outsourced services. The SFO's CEO must demand great execution and service, and identify other companies and relationships to call on if necessary by annually soliciting requests for proposals (RFPs) from several outstanding firms.

Negotiate the fees of outside providers and services, and demand the best prices for commodity services, which, after all, are all about the price.

Enterprising CEOs often find outside providers through their extensive and influential networks among families, other SFO executives and leaders in areas such as finance, legal, accounting, politics and consulting. Especially in a "growing wealth" CEO role, these networks are incredibly valuable. A customer relationship management computer program (CRM) and other database management systems can help the SFO remain active with the best influencers in their network.

Finding the best talent, aligned with the family mission, the CEO's leadership and the culture is the key to creating an effective family office environment. Each hire should be carefully considered for skills, incentives and growth opportunities. Strive to create a team that's really driven by a shared vision and goals.

Next, top leaders and talent must develop a brand that the family will find fresh and relevant. Chapter 7 shows family office leaders how to accomplish that in a way that honors the family's unique culture and that will serve their ever-evolving needs.

7

Branding: A Cultural Imperative

"Culture eats strategy for breakfast."

— PETER DRUCKER

The pieces are starting to fall into place. Governance, leadership, culture, talent— these are all components that help build the brand of the family office to secure the buy-in of the family it serves. Only with this buy-in and support will the family office be able to executive effectively and sustainably. The family office brand can be seen as the sum total of the felt experiences of the family the SFO serves. Family members may perceive that their SFO reliably and dependably delivers "functional services" (investment advice, wealth transfer, tax arbitrage, etc.). Today, say Matt Wesley, Dana Green and John Wong[7], these attributes are simply the brand's ante—its cost of entry. They are not sufficient to *differentiate* the family office brand and secure its spot in family members' hearts and minds.

While there are many definitions of brand, the definition I prefer comes from Marty Neumeier's seminal book, "The Brand Gap." Neumeier posits that the brand is "the gut feeling a person has about a product, service or organization." This means that brand is only partially under a family office's control. As Neumeier says, "A brand is not what you say it is, but what THEY say it is." We must redefine brands not as logos such as the Nike swoosh, but as sets of cognitive and emotional associations in

---

7 Family Office Association white paper, "Playing Ball on Running Water: The Strategic Importance of Human Resources for SFOs."

customers' (and even non-customers') heads. Together, these associations make up a brand's meaning. Companies can have brands, but so can people and places. When client experience is aggregated, what emerges is the brand. In short, brands are any associations that consumers (in this case, family members) care about. Today, clients and customers control that conversation.

FAMILY EXPERIENCE IS THE NEW SFO BRANDING IMPERATIVE

Lou Carbone, world-renowned customer experience management thought leader, points out that every customer (for our purpose, family member) has an experience with your company. All family members interacting with the SFO have their own personal experience every time they make contact. In his book, "Clued In: How to Keep Customers Coming Back Again and Again" (FT Press, 2004), Carbone explains, "Taking that personal connection out of the business, whether in the name of greater efficiency or due to a simple lack of awareness, reduces the business to a sterile exercise in mathematics: how much, by how many, how fast, or how big a return. There's no passion or pride in that way of doing business. There's no soul. Ultimately, there's no lasting value for customers."

To make customers (for the SFO, family members) elated, let alone satisfied, he says, "Hiring, education and training, marketing, facility design, incentives, measurement, and communications will all need to be aligned and synchronized to deliver on deep-seated customer needs and desires ... Literally everyone from chief executive officers and chief experience officers to unit managers and team leaders are beginning to wrestle with the common issues around customer experience as a value proposition."

There are three keys to creating a perpetually powerful SFO-branded family experience:

1) *Identify* family delights and disappointments (emotional) and uncover unmet needs (functional);

2) *Design* specific and intentional experiences that leverage the brand's story and core competencies; and

3) *Build* a family community that shapes conversations already happening between the family, influencers and the brand. These conversations are particularly intimate and important within the family. They are also the lifeblood of a successful SFO.

Carbone suggests that experiences can be designed, but most companies lack the skills, experience and methodologies to take charge of that design. They struggle with how to manage or intentionally deliver experiences that create highly positive interactions and maximum value for customers. Businesses are increasingly warming to the idea that the quality of the experience is inextricably linked to building long-term loyalty, not in just the quantity of touch points or even in the brilliance of the offered counsel. In short, a brand today is not what company says it is, but rather how, in our case, the family experiences the intersection of family and SFO cultures.

SFO leadership must deploy effective diagnostics to uncover the culture of the family and how the family actually experiences the SFO brand. Understanding the full family office experience requires tapping into each represented generation. After this assessment and benchmarking, the SFO must design new family experiences that reinforce the SFO brand, which defines not only service offerings but also appropriate service boundaries and the accompanying desired emotional connection. Next, the SFO must extend the influence and reach of these designed experiences to all family members, as well as external constituencies and stakeholders, in order to reinforce the SFO's story to social influencers at large. This, say Wesley, Green and Wong, brings us to the level of strategy.

THE FAMILY VERSUS FAMILY OFFICE CULTURE

It's important to note that the family office's culture is distinct from the family's culture. Matt Wesley, Dana Green and John Wong explain that many SFO personnel believe their firm's culture is the same as that of the family they serve. This creates a significant blind spot to their own "operating system." Other SFO personnel may be able to point to elements of their unique culture, but few truly understand it. Family members also often do not distinguish their own culture from their SFO's. These blind spots of both family and the SFO can wreak havoc on both.

As a starting point, it is important to recognize that the family and the SFO serve two vastly different missions. Every family's mission rests on a core cultural imperative of inclusion. Every SFO's mission, on the other hand, revolves around generating cultures of performance. Family leaders and their SFO CEO must learn how to make these two imperatives coexist in order to operate smoothly and effectively.

Angelo Robles

SETTING LEADERSHIP EXPECTATIONS

SFO executives must clarify the brand expectations of the family and work effectively with family governance structures to design and deliver a positive brand experience. The SFO must also help family governance structures understand defined boundaries, and enforce them within the family. The SFO will no longer be all things to all people. If and when the family clamors for brand dilution, SFO leaders must stand up to the initial resistance and harness support from family leadership.

Sometimes a period of transition can be rocky, but if the initial assessments hit the mark and the family experience is designed collaboratively and with a view to creating emotional connection with the brand promise, then this period can be short. During this transition, firm leadership will need "cover" from family leaders. It is more likely that the firm leadership will be able to attain this coverage if the family leaders possess both strategic clarity and buy-in on the intentional design parameters.

First, the family culture and the culture of the SFO must be assessed both quantitatively and qualitatively. This assessment must be benchmarked where possible and must contain a deep analysis of core competencies and breakpoints within both the firm and family culture to determine where opportunities lie.

Second, the family experience must be intentionally designed, deployed and refined. Family experience cannot be left to drift. Leaderships of both the SFO and the family must collaborate to create clear boundaries around what the family office promises to deliver and how to set extraordinarily high expectations within those boundaries. This will often require political cover in the period of transition as the family adjusts its expectations that the family office cannot be all things to all people but will deliver exceptional experiences in what it has committed to do. Once deployed, delivering family experience within brand promise requires ongoing learning and feedback in a process of continual improvement.

Third, and perhaps most important, human resources practices must be attuned to the brand promise and delivery of exceptional client experience. In this sense, human resources will be elevated to a strategic level. Wesley, Green and Wong explain that this should be done with a view to enhancing brand experience. HR leadership will manage and review staff with a view to the experience of the family. Leaders of the SFO will focus on the felt experiences in both cultures and develop key metrics

48

to measure performance. They will gear evaluations and compensation toward the creation of exceptional experiences in both cultures.

As an example, let's look at the culture of the University of Alabama's premier college football team, built by Head Coach Nick Saban. The university's athletic director oversees Coach Saban, who ultimately answers to the University President. Both bosses give the coach the resources and support that he needs to succeed. Saban demands perfection and expects a national championship every year. He's extremely dedicated to the "process," consistently hires the best people for assistant coaches, including former NFL and top college coaches. Nothing is left to chance. The team's athletic trainer is the best paid in college football. This top-down organization is completely dedicated to winning (its singular goal).

For a family or its SFO, great organizational culture and talent endure and innovate even as family members, goals and resulting SFO deliverables change over time. The foundation of a great company is built upon leadership, culture and the right talent, managed well. The right culture and people will always strive for the best answer if you build this into the family's and SFO's mantra and DNA. Staff and leadership will effectively and efficiently source information and resources that lead to the best decisions. No sacred cows are allowed, no egos. It's all about the best answer, no matter the source.

In Chapter 8 we explore how to honor the past, understand the present and prepare for an uncertain future.

8

Past, Present and Future: Succession Planning

"There's the business you're in, and the business you're becoming. If you just manage the business you're in, you're going to get knocked out by a new technology or new competition. But if you're constantly managing those two businesses, you won't have to pivot, because you're always doing something to innovate, or to change or to improve."

—TONY ROBBINS, *INC* MAGAZINE, OCTOBER 2016

Great SFO leaders act in the present, but build toward the future by hiring, training and managing (overseeing) the right talent. They also respect and harness the family's past—its history, accomplishments, traditions, values and legacy. Without this holistic approach, even a family office that looks good on paper might be doomed to fail.

HONORING AND LEARNING FROM THE PAST

Often the first-generation wealth creator is strongly determined to have the SFO succeed and to achieve family harmony and a unifying vision. As the second generation comes of age and gains power and influence, their interest in family harmony is often not as strong as the first generation's. It's very hard to hold true to a clear vision of the SFO, an empowered CEO, and positive culture and talent working together, when family members of influence have competing goals and desires.

DEVELOPING CORE COMPETENCIES

Matt Wesley of the Merrill Lynch Center for Family Wealth and Governance has developed twelve core competencies that he finds necessary to secure the human, social and cultural capital of families, which in turn form the basis for family success over time. These competencies include: communication, shared vision, fostering family legacy, history, education and leadership among all generations, trust, complete transparency, and what we call adaptive governance.

Destruction from within is a far more common cause of dissipation of family wealth than ineffective planning. Intra-family litigation is likely to erupt over time if significant attention, communication and progress are not dedicated to the competencies Wesley identifies. The only way the second generation will embrace collaborative decision-making, Wesley believes, is for the first generation to model it.

As the saying "shirtsleeves to shirtsleeves in three generations" implies, the first generation all too often creates the wealth, only for the second generation to coast on the status quo and stagnation, followed by the dissipation of wealth in the third generation.

James Hughes's seminal work, "Family Wealth: Keeping It in the Family" (Bloomberg Press, 2004), explains that families are far more than financial capital. They also possess human capital, cultural capital and social capital. It takes coordination of all types of family capital to preserve financial capital over subsequent generations. Hughes emphasizes that family members would be wise to address qualitative questions such as:

- Is each individual family member thriving?
- Does the social compact among the members of each generation provide incentive to the leaders of each generation to stay actively engaged in the family?
- Do family leaders listen to the individual issues of those they lead, so those members will choose to follow?
- Are selected representatives of the family meeting their responsibilities to manage the family's human, intellectual and financial capital in order to achieve the individual pursuits of happiness of each of its family members?
- Does each member perceive that family leaders are doing so effectively?

Discussing these questions, perhaps at a family meeting, will go a long way towards helping the family take a long-term holistic approach to managing their financial, legal, investment and other issues. Such discussions help the family avoid the shirtsleeves to shirtsleeves in three generations paradigm.

Constant changes in the internal, as well as external, environment can either spark dynamic engagement among family members or impose dangerous minefields that will likely damage not only the SFO, but the family as well.

Wonderful leaders encourage family leaders, board members and employees to ask questions and challenge assumptions. They encourage debate about ideas and direction.

In their book "The Founder's Mentality: How to Overcome the Predictable Crises of Growth" (Harvard Review Press, 2016), Chris Zook and James Allen of consulting firm Bain & Co. have identified three primary traits they call the "founder's mentality." These traits propel a burgeoning family business to another level, progressing toward greatness. These traits are absolutely essential in the CEO of an SFO as well:

- A sense of insurgent mission, characterized by a sense of higher purpose and a long-term horizon.
- An obsession with the front line, characterized by an intellectual curiosity about every detail of the customer experience of how everything in the business works. Executives use instincts formed at the ground level to make every decision; frontline employees are empowered and are the heroes of the business; and the customer voice is central to all decisions.
- A powerful sense of responsibility for employees, customers, products and decisions, characterized by an antipathy to bureaucracy and a bias toward speed in decisions and actions.

These traits will help the SFO devote its resources to the family's most important goals and build superior capabilities internally when possible and outsource the rest to organizations that can deliver exceptional services in the other areas. Creating a "stop doing" list can help keep the team—from top down—focused.

SFOs, which usually have a limited number of employees and bureaucracy, should be highly creative, nimble, and effective. Somehow, though, effectiveness and leadership are often lacking.

When family leaders feel their SFO is not exceptional, they need to face reality. Are the family and SFO leaders able to confront problems about vision, leadership, culture and talent head on? Can family leaders harness the desire and determination to make their SFO exceptional? Do they apply maximum resources to the best opportunities (per the goals of the family)? Are family members engaged?

In some cases, a prudent board, a resolution committee, and perhaps an internal SFO "fixer" can address problems, clearing the way for the talent to focus on opportunities and best-in-class execution and service of the family's goals.

WAVE OF THE FUTURE

Great CEOs articulate the need for and help build the SFO's management succession plan without feeling that it's a threat to their future role. Quite the contrary: by building the resources that ensure smooth succession, they increase their own value. CEOs who don't do so contribute to the eventual downfall of the SFO, especially as the family grows and expands over time, and family members develop conflicting interests. One of the most important ways to pave the way for families to thrive across generations is to develop a clear succession plan that anticipates changes in the family composition and needs.

9

Financial Considerations

"An SFO exists primarily to centralize, preserve and transfer significant family wealth across generations while at the same time acting as an effective inter-generational safeguard and touchstone for the family's collective values, aspirations, heritage and legacy."

—MARC HALSEMA, ADVISOR, GLOBAL FAMILY OFFICES

Once the family office is established, it's time to turn the attention to deliverables. The most common mandate of an SFO is to sustain the dynastic wealth, resources and legacy through the generations—most simply, wealth preservation. In other words, the family is in the stay-rich business.

Whether you're overhauling an existing or launching a new SFO, jurisdictional issues, intertwining of ownership, legal entities and tax considerations are integral to this process. Varying family assets, issues and concerns, and country-specific domicile decisions will dictate the choices about structures and agreements. Often, assets are held in various individual, trust and organizational entities, in which the asset owners enter into an agreement to manage those assets with the management company/SFO, which is compensated by the asset owners. This structure, depending on ownership of the management company/SFO (progressively in the U.S. an Alaska LLC with decision to tax as a c-corp), usually allows the most capable tax advantages[8] for potentially

---

8 This is a HIGHLY complex subject requiring highly competent legal and accounting counsel who are experienced in SFOs.

deducting the management costs of the assets and services rendered. This can be a powerful advantage of an SFO. The prospective deductibility of certain expenses must be structured in a way to allow such advantages. In addition to investment services, the SFO should have a clear and preferably diverse business purpose (accounting, reporting services, etc.). The asset-owning entities, no matter how many, should each have their own agreements with the SFO or other management company.

GLOBAL CUSTODIANSHIP/JURISDICTIONS

As many wealthy families own substantial publicly traded equities, an SFO must diversify custodial risks of the organizations that transact and report on those equities. SFOs should have multiple custodians carefully vetted for financial strength and digital security protocols. These custodians should be geographically diverse. It's important to locate jurisdictional domiciles in a variety of safe countries (considered by many to include the United States, Canada, Switzerland, Singapore, Malta, New Zealand and Australia). SFOs and families should factor in travel access and security, privacy protocols, contract law, custody options and talent, especially if the family is headquartered in a less-stable geographic or political environment. Government confiscation through taxation, runaway inflation (non-dollar currency), and political and regulatory risks can be very real.

Wealthy global citizens are frequently and rightfully concerned about how their families are or may be impacted by increased governmental regulation, and the greater use of technology and resources shared among governments. SFOs must be extremely sophisticated in their approach to managing tax exposure—globally— now more than ever before. It's also imperative to proactively make use of a variety of advanced strategies maximizing intellectual property (IP) interests domiciled offshore in tax-favored jurisdictions, intra-family entities engaged with family loan structures, carried interest opportunities, depreciation (on real estate, aircraft and certain other assets), and investment and foreign tax credits usage, coordinated with tax-free investments.

Given the exceptional importance of tax arbitrage and flexibility of jurisdictional fluidity, an individual or family of great wealth can take an immediate tax hit and move to or domicile in a country (certain countries like the U.S. make this very difficult for existing citizens without renouncing citizenship) with little or even no income and/or capital gains taxes (particularly on out-of-country sourced income or investments).

Depending on the impact of taxes on their particular business interests and holdings, they would simply own and direct resources (now with a clean tax slate) in tax favorable jurisdictions.

Such families could travel frequently around the world, somewhat as global citizens. U.S. citizens can obtain some of these tax benefits, by moving their personal residence of domicile and business interest(s) to two specific U.S. territories with extraordinary tax benefits (as of this writing): Puerto Rico and the U.S. Virgin Islands.

Of course, implementing these techniques may raise some psychological challenges as well as family issues, which could hamper family buy-in.

Related to this technique is choosing where to base a virtual family office. Official domicile and ownership of the SFO and any intertwining agreements with entities that own family assets are critical to maximize long-term tax benefits (as described earlier in this chapter). Today's resources, including technology, virtual reality (VR), artificial intelligence (AI), globalization trends and outsourcing, enable family offices to be more fluid and nimble than ever before. VR over the next several years will be game changing and revolutionary.

In reality, even billionaires are at the whim of the government and what they say and make us do. James Rickards paints a scary scenario about what he calls a "shadow struggle" between sovereign and corporate power. In his book "The Road to Ruin: The Global Elites' Secret Plan for the Next Financial Crisis" (Portfolio, 2016), he explains, "Sovereign power always wins in the end because countries have decisive tools, including violence. Still, corporate capacity to corrupt a country through lobbying is sufficient in the short run to fend off state power. In a decentralized system of high-tax developed countries and low-tax haven countries, global corporations easily find ways to avoid taxation."

The SFO CEO must evaluate how such risks affect exceptionally wealthy families and their ability to remain in the "stay-rich business." This requires the CEO to coordinate with internal and external family resources, including advanced, competent and diverse legal and tax experts who are experienced in the complexities of wealthy families, as well as the intricacies of varying global domiciles and the interplay of family "ownership interests" of trusts, trustees, corporations, partnerships and foundations.

A FAMILY OFFICE INVESTING PRIMER

Every family needs an investment policy statement, known as an IPS. A clear and con-cise written document defining financial goals and expectations, an IPS outlines asset classes allowable to invest in, expected range of percentages to invest in such asset classes, risk tolerance, timeline, liquidity desires, limitations on certain investments, and other parameters the chairman, investment committee and CIO desire as perti-nent. The IPS details the type of asset allocation the chairman, investment committee and CIO believe is best to execute upon the investment goals of the family.

Before I go further I'll reiterate what I've stated many times: a family of truly great wealth does not necessarily need to invest, at least not in the short-term, or even per-haps the mid-to long-term. The default option is always cash!

Some families follow a classic strategic asset allocation (setting target allocations and percentages to various asset classes and periodically rebalancing to maintain the standard set in the IPS); others are perhaps more tactical, allowing more freedom on the ranges or percentages of allocations to various asset classes depending on market conditions at the moment, per the investment committee's or CIO's discretion. Some follow a more goals-driven allocation, in that there are eight, 10, 20 or more goals, and each goal deserves its own IPS and asset allocation approach. Another common approach is known as core-satellite: the core part of the portfolio construction follows a more strategic allocation approach, while a smaller percentage is dedicated more tactically to asset classes and specific investments more volatile, such that a more active approach may produce "alpha" (excessive returns generated by the skill of the investor).

Author Nassim Taleb advocates what he calls a barbell approach: a majority of the allocation and underlying securities selection is very conservative and highly liq-uid, while a smaller allocation is highly tactical and rather aggressive, with nothing in between.

From a decision on allocation—and there are amazing investors who practice all these approaches (they all can work)—follows security selection. This comes down to a preference for either a more passive or a more active approach and should be noted in the IPS. Some investors strongly prefer a passive approach, believing that, net of fees and taxes, it's hard to beat the market and, therefore, an indexing-like approach is best, at least for public securities. Others take a more active approach, believing that investment skill can make a difference and that more active security selection, whether in-house or through third-party managers, even net of fees and taxes, can produce superior returns. Many family offices pursue a combination of these approaches, similar to the core-satellite approach.

Some SFOs that embrace a passive approach nevertheless choose to own the underlying securities, not through fund or ETF, however directly, they control the tax picture completely for tax-loss harvesting and can screen out select securities that, perhaps for social reasons, they prefer not to invest in. This gives the most transparency.

Others are more active in their approach, choosing third party managers they believe provide an edge, and get superior returns, net of fees (but with less control of the tax picture), and will continue to do so. Some refer to this as an endowment investing approach: the SFO is focused on the IPS and asset allocation strategy (and hiring and firing managers), but leaves the securities decisions to third party managers they deem skilled in getting alpha.

Never forget to really look at the full picture: it's not gross returns, it's net of fees and taxes that really matters. And, of course, other aspects matter along with investment return—including transparency, liquidity, risks being taken to achieve higher returns, etc.

Many families lately have taken a more active role in direct investing in private companies. Feeling confident in their edge in a particular industry or their own overall business acumen, in a less efficient industry than public companies, creates more opportunity for alpha. Along with this, and somewhat depending on whether a controlling or non-controlling interest, comes greater influence on the direction of the management of the company and transparency on their insights. In addition, unlike being a limited partner (LP) investor, such as through a hedge fund or private equity fund, you as an investor will have a say in when to exit the company.

Some families co-invest in direct deals with other families. Others take this to another level and create what some describe as consortiums: families of great wealth coming together to form an investment company, sharing resources and talent to collectively invest more strategically and retain more control, compared to private equity fund investing.

Although not defined as a separate asset class, some families also invest in alternatives such as hedge funds. Hedge funds may have the freedom to pursue pure alpha as the portfolio manager (PM) deems applicable and not be constrained in their choices of what to invest in by traditional mandates. They can also implement short ideas (meaning investing in companies they believe that their stock value will decline and they are investing hoping and expecting this to happen), others may use leverage and other advanced strategies such as derivatives.

Recently, net of fees, hedge funds have underperformed. Additionally, they often provide, for many, a poor tax-control picture (for the private non-tax-free investor). That said, many investors believe that a certain allocation to managers who truly know how to hedge—living up to the moniker "hedge funds"—can make sense in a defensive portfolio.

Every family has different goals, risk tolerances, timelines and liquidity needs. Based on my belief in generational wealth preservation as the No. 1 objective for most families of wealth, below is a very general perspective on an allocation profile:

- 20 percent in cash (diverse global currencies)
- 20 percent in public company stocks (purchased through and held by globally diverse brokerages/custodians)
- 10 percent in income-generating private companies
- 10 percent in bonds
- 10 percent in true hedge funds
- 10 percent in income-generating real estate
- 5 percent in actual gold and silver (some kept outside the U.S. and even the banking system)
- 5 percent in farmland
- 5 percent in startups, angel and venture
- 3 percent in high-quality art
- 2 percent in high-quality diamonds, including colored diamonds

Such diversity in allocation—let alone underlying securities, cash and company selection—is often not best to maximize potential returns. Such diversity is meant to hedge and manage long-term risks. Again, this is about wealth preservation.

Many families of wealth, often encouraged by younger family members, believe that they need to be more socially aware of the impact of their investing on society and causes near and dear to them; this approach is defined as impact investing. Underlying security selection that remains within the parameters of the family's beliefs is paramount.

For families or CEOs following the endowment model of investing, of choosing outside managers/funds to implement on their IPS and asset allocation strategy, it's critical to build the investment resources of the SFO around this focus.

Families focused on direct investing (although many families are a combination of both), need resources and talent that has more investment banking and private equity experiences, this is often at a premium. If a family elects to play in this arena, they need to come prepared and ready to build a true investment company. This takes time, talent and money. This relates to the importance of aligned interest and limiting conflicts of interest in the SFO.

Particularly for those focused on direct investing, to attract top talent, the family must compensate talent as the markets determine; factors to consider include compensation provided by hedge funds, PE funds and top investment banks. Compensation will revolve around more than base salary, and commonly includes co-investing opportunity. Families do need to be aware that often their long-term interests may differ from the often short-term horizons of their SFO executives!

It is very important to manage compensation in a way that helps align interests and is understanding of and empathetic to the needs of talent in top professions. Bonuses with gross-ups (or perhaps forgivable loans), allowing the SFO's investing-focused executives to co-invest, perhaps phantom interest as opposed to an actual interest in the deal, deferred compensation and applicable to the family, golden handcuff strategies—all are useful compensation metrics and negotiation points.

No matter a family's investing focus, extreme care and diligence must be exercised at all times to manage expectations and desired results. Ownership structures (and domicile) of such actual investments, maximizing tax and wealth transfer planning, as well as intertwined agreements with the ownership of the SFO management entity are crucial to the long-term success and maximum net of tax true returns.

The family, its advisors and the CEO of their SFO should carefully coordinate the intertwined tax and estate plans and asset-protection benefits of the family's trusts, corporations, partnerships, foundations and, of course, the SFO. Depending on tax domicile, the most expensive aspect of the SFO is frequently its employees, a cost that may be deductible to the tax-paying family. Legal and tax professionals of exceptional talent who are experienced in family and SFO matters should guide decisions about ownership structure of the SFO and the structure of the assets it manages. These experts should factor in proper jurisdictional considerations to achieve favorable tax benefits for the family.

PRIVATE TRUST COMPANIES

A Private Trust Company (PTC), commonly a special purpose trust, can hold and manage (as a trustee) various family trusts, entities and resources. Depending on domicile, PTCs can have an unlimited lifespan. Family members and non-family members may hold various positions within the PTC. A PTC can own and act as the trustee of unique non-liquid assets (such as land or businesses) in situations where a trusted outside trustee is difficult to source. Most elegantly, PTCs institutionalize multigenerational wealth by ensuring continuity of the management of said assets along with the seamless intergenerational transfer of assets. The PTC structure even allows active family members to acquire errors and omissions insurance to hedge against possible fiduciary risks and liabilities.

A STRONG BACK OFFICE

Many SFOs overlook or wrongly undervalue services such as aggregation and reporting of family assets, payroll, bill pay, household management services, security and medical coordination, as well as all-important IT and cyber-security. These, like every service the SFO performs for the family, should be measured for effectiveness against a high standard benchmark of expectations. Every SFO policy and procedures manual should specify strict office protocols and mechanics regarding cash management, distributions and wires, as well as internal and external auditing procedures.

SFOs with diverse alternative investments and LP interests may greatly benefit by engaging the services and resources of fund administrators, hedging services and other "middle-office services."

Whichever investment strategies an SFO pursues, it will be impossible to enhance and preserve dynastic wealth in today's world without embracing new technology. Chapter 10 shows how technology can help the family office become effective, resilient and adaptive, and points out some new risks of the digital world.

10

The Technology Factor

"Inefficiencies make sustainable successful businesses very hard."

—JAY ABRAHAM, CONSULTANT

Technological advancement is already impacting families of wealth, family offices and the advisors who service them. An effective family office embraces technology and keeps an eye on the horizon of innovation. In the future, advances will enable artificial intelligence (AI), machine learning algorithms, virtual reality (VR) and robotics to do more and more, and do it more effectively and cost efficiently for corporations and family offices. Allow us to quickly delve into the technologies that are not only on the horizon but actually emerging around us every day.

AI services are beginning to replace more traditional investment advisors for the mass affluent and many of their traditional services, including asset allocation, security selection and tax loss harvesting. "Robo advisors" can already select investment allocations, decide which equity and bond index funds to buy and sell, and maximize tax-loss harvesting more effectively than most human advisors.

VR will revolutionize the way businesses and SFOs assess, engage, hire and train employees. In the future, staff will "be there without being there," no longer tied to a physical location. This will open up an employee universe of disparate geographic talent, which will be better sourced, managed and trained than ever before.

Though it may seem early for a discussion on these technologies and their impact on the SFO field, we refer back to Tony Robbins's quote that encourages us to be forward-looking in our businesses.

VR is in its infancy in terms of practicality, but will likely advance even more quickly than AI, actively changing the white-collar workforce. Oculus, Microsoft HoloLens and gaming powerhouse Valve are among the leaders in VR (as of this writing) and appear to be on the cusp of significant advancement.

As with AI and technology in general, investment opportunities will abound for some families and SFOs. Others will see the value of utilizing VR to enhance globalization of the SFO workforce, training and education in general, and a more immersive engagement with disperse providers. In the not-too-distant future—and straight out of movies such as "Minority Report" and the "Iron Man" series—VR headsets, followed by glasses and eventually contact lenses, will replace the need for TVs and computer displays.

Not to be outdone, AI will eventually have an even greater impact. Andrew Ng, Chief Scientist at Baidu Research, labels AI the "new electricity." Driverless vehicles will significantly impact employment, insurance, city land usage and traffic. Surgery is one of many highly-skilled tasks that AI will simply do better, in time, than humans. It's hard to imagine a profession other than those requiring extreme creativity and the arts that won't be affected in the coming decades. Investment opportunities and success for a small group of entrepreneurs in AI, machine learning algorithms and VR have the potential to create the first trillion-dollar individual.

Technology companies like Google and its DeepMind AI are making astonishing progress as aggregators and interpreters of big data into predictive analytics and, being machine learning, it simply improves upon this process. Exceptional financial firms Bridgewater and Blackrock have also been proactive in building out their AI/machine learning algorithms. Legendary investor Steve Cohen recently opened a venture capital firm in Silicon Valley and hired top-tier experts to invest in promising AI and machine learning startups.

One of the most exciting technology developments is bitcoin and its underlying blockchain technology, which Don and Alex Tapscott, authors of "Blockchain Revolution: How the Technology Behind Bitcoin is Changing Money, Business and the World" (Portfolio, 2016), describe as "an incorruptible digital ledger of economic transactions that can be programmed to record not just financial transactions but virtually everything of value." Blockchain offers the first truly decentralized, distributed ledger for record-keeping; it can be used to track financial transactions, digital stock certificates, insurance claims and voting systems, as well as birth, marriage and death certificates.

In their book, the Tapscotts explain, "If business, government, and civil society innovators get this right, we will move from an internet driven primarily by falling costs of search, coordination, data collection, and decision making—where the name of the game was monitoring, mediating, and monetizing information and transactions on the Web—to one driven by the falling costs of bargaining, policing, and enforcing social and commercial agreements, where the name of the game will be integrity, security, collaboration, the privacy of all transactions, and the creation and distribution of value."

We must consider these new technologies and their impact on the world around us from the perspective of the two main risks to family offices: Many SFOs are very outdated and must work hard to get up to speed, and many advances can impose speed bumps that can be as disruptive as they are helpful.

GETTING UP TO SPEED

Many SFO executives are over 50, members of an age group that tends to be less techno-savvy than younger generations brought up using smartphones, laptops and social media. While it's certainly possible to outsource many digital services such as tax management, financial aggregation and cybersecurity, if an SFO has no one on staff who is knowledgeable and comfortable with the world of technology, including VR and AI, the office may not be able to select and oversee trustworthy and effective vendors.

Thinking back to our chapter on a diverse workplace, we see that the key is balance when it comes to technology, too. SFOs need older, experienced leaders and staff who comprehend the complex concerns and needs of the family, who have navigated both up and down economic cycles, and who are comfortable and proficient with softer people issues such as family dynamics and systems. But, especially when it comes to wealth preservation, an SFO that wants to maximize effectiveness and build a sustainable organization would be wise to hire young, diverse, vibrant people who are native to ever-evolving technologies.

SPEED TRAPS

Despite all the exciting promises of these innovations, SFOs, like other organizations, can become slaves to technology. It's important not to jump into what seem to be easy-to-use technologies that provide value and increase effectiveness without exploring potential risks and drawbacks.

For instance, if you're highly concerned about things like aggregation, which reveals what you own to the aggregation company, then you may be more comfortable using Excel spreadsheets, at least in the short term. If you worry about cybersecurity, you may shy away from Cloud storage. But eventually, it will become almost impossible to operate an outdated, "on paper" SFO in a digital world. The trick is to be aware of the vulnerabilities new technologies may create and know how to track and address those risks.

- *Privacy and Safety.* One of the biggest security threats presented by the wave of technology is in the cyber realm. Author James Rickards points out that hacking can wreak havoc on critical infrastructure, such as dams, power grids and stock markets. The result could be floods, blackouts and viruses. For instance, a sleeper attack virus in 2010 was planted in the NASDAQ's operating system by Russian military intelligence. Although the virus was disabled, Rickards says, "No one knows how many undiscovered digital viruses are lying in wait."
- *Cloud versus Outsourced Data Storage.* The family and SFO must decide how to store and manage their data and information. For instance, does the SFO utilize an internal server or the Cloud? Each has advantages and disadvantages. The Cloud is widely accepted, efficient and cost-effective, and it's a convenient solution. However, it creates various privacy concerns. At the time of this writing, information stored on the Cloud of an outsourced provider domiciled within the United States is subject to government subpoena of the Cloud provider. In such cases, the provider would have to comply and turn over requested information to the government; however, the provider is not under any requirement to inform its client, the data owner, of such a transfer of information.

Families and SFOs that consider privacy of utmost importance may prefer the extra expense, time and effort required to install a private server. Going to further extremes, SFOs may wish to explore the privacy laws of varying countries and consider intertwining ownership entities and domicile of IP, data and information in an offshore destination with exceptional 24/7 security (keeping in mind, of course, that even that could be subject to breach).

SFOs need to explore, thoroughly understand and make strategic decisions about technological services that aggregate and report on their assets. Clearly tracking the exact and immediate value of liquid securities and the tax-holding periods of assets allows the SFO to proactively and more conveniently manage tax implications and varying risk metrics on public securities. Many, if not most, family offices do not currently outsource aggregation and reporting services. Instead, they elect to perform these functions internally, using custom Microsoft Excel spreadsheets in coordination with the reports they receive from their custodians, to manage the aggregation and reporting to the family. Some do this more effectively than others. However, while this strategy provides more internal control and privacy, even those who execute internal aggregation and reporting activities well rarely have the firepower to do more immediate risk analysis.

12 TIPS TO MITIGATE YOUR ONLINE RISK

Derived from conversations between Russell Greer, Founder of Control Key and Angelo Robles at the 2017 FOA Miami with additional details provided for this book.

1. **NEVER Give Information to Companies that Call You**
   You should not believe a person who calls and claims to be from a company like Microsoft or Apple (or any other company with which you have an account). Callers might sound convincing and may attempt to direct you to log-me-in, team-viewer, or some other IT tool for remote management. These are fraudulent calls! Hang up immediately, without answering questions or providing information and call your IT Department. **Companies will NEVER call to ask you for your information.**

2. **ALWAYS Backup Your Data Using the 3-2-1 Model**
   Backup your data frequently, 24-hour backups are advisable (Apple users can use the built-in functionality of Time Machine as a safety, but should

consider additional backups that are managed). When you create backups you should have:

- **3** copies of your data, on
- **2** different media types, in at least
- **1** remote location

3. **ENABLE Full-disk Encryption**

Encryption is an added layer of protection for your data, and most devices now have built-in encryption tools. Apple users should enable FileVault and Windows users can use BitLocker to easily encrypt data.

4. **LIMIT Admin Rights and Review Frequently**

Disable administrative rights for users who don't require access. The more accounts with admin rights, the greater your risk.

- Escalate privileges only when absolutely necessary for an employee to do their job.
- Create a special admin-user account for running updates or installing software/peripherals, etc.
- Modify your regular user profile to a "standard" user role.
- Do a monthly review to ensure admin access is appropriately assigned (remove anyone who no longer needs admin rights).
- *Immediately* remove anyone who leaves the organization from any administrative rights (or otherwise) within your system.

5. **RUN Anti-Virus Software on All Devices**

Anti-virus software should be installed on all devices and run in real-time to mitigate risk. Use the daily full scan feature to ensure full protection.

6. **INSTALL Malware Prevention Software on All Devices**

MalwareBytes or WebRoot are currently good solutions to prevent malware infections, ensure "real-time protection" is enabled and review the scan reports daily.

7. **ENABLE Automatic Software Updates**

Software providers continuously provide updates and patches to their pro-grams to fix any vulnerabilities. Enable automatic updates on third-party software to ensure all your workstations, laptops and other computers are protected.

8. **SEPARATE Personal and Work Data**

   Limit the risk to your professional data by using separate devices for personal tasks.

9. **PROTECT Your Devices**

   Do not let others use your work devices – even your children. Work devices should be used solely by employees at all times. While the person using your device may not have any ill intention they could open you to risk by clicking links or installing programs.

10. **IMPLEMENT Password Standards**

    Create rules for password creation that include strength requirements, frequency of updates (at a minimum ever 42 days), etc. Remove any passwords stored in files on your computer or in the cloud unless they are in an explicit, trusted password protection program like Keepass (standalone version). Rules to follow include:

    • Do not use the same passwords across your personal and professional life
    • Do not use the same passwords across different websites
    • Do not reuse passwords on websites
    • Do not include birthdays or family names in your passwords (children, spouse, etc.)
    • Longer passwords are always safer
    • Include non-standard characters and capitalization when you are able

11. **ENABLE Two-Factor Authentication and Prevent Porting**

    Two-factor authentication is an added layer of protection that requires not only a username and password but also an additional piece of information that only the user could have (like a code sent to a mobile phone). Most cloud services allow you to enable two-factor – you should activate it on all email accounts and social media accounts.

    If you do enable two-factor authentication, contact your phone service provider and let them know that your phone number should **not be ported** (forwarded to another device) without you personally doing so in a store with photo ID. Porting phone numbers is the newest risk vector so ensure you are protected.

12. USE Caution When Opening Email

Review emails carefully before opening them. If your email provider gives you a warning on the email, use extra caution and perhaps contact your IT department for guidance.

- Never assume that the name in the "from" field is real – this is easy to manipulate
- Do NOT open attachments of ANY kind unless you know the sender AND are expecting the attachment
- Ask for guidance from IT or knowledgeable friends before opening anything that you are suspicious of – better safe than sorry.
- Consider contacting the sender via phone if you have any doubts to inquire about the email to ensure its authenticity

DISRUPTION IN THE WORKFORCE.

Eventually, when AI is able to do many tasks better than humans, we will face a potential jobless society that could cause grave challenges and perhaps civil unrest and chaos. Of course, in the foreseeable future, AI and VR will not be able to supplant human emotional intelligence, creativity and innovation, or coordination with human co-workers, which will become even more important than ever to execute and continually service the goals of the family. However, even in the shorter term, VR, AI and machine learning algorithms could enable SFOs to decrease the number of people needed to accomplish their goals.

What might this mean, eventually, when AI will be able to do nearly any task better than humans? At the macro level, one potential scenario might be a jobless society that could pose difficult choices that may or may not result in massive unemployment and could, as mentioned, cause civil unrest and chaos. At the micro level, wealthy families would be wise to have their SFO devote substantial resources to preserving wealth over the generations. Education, focusing on a positive vision of the future and investing in a civil society through philanthropy can, to a degree, help hedge against many future dangers to the family and the social order.

PROCESSES TO CONSIDER AUTOMATING

Keeping in mind the benefits and risks of new technologies, SFOs may want to consider how some high-tech services and products can be valuable. In "Idea to Execution: How to Optimize, Automate and Outsource Everything in Your Business" (Lioncrest Publishing, 2016), authors Ari Meisel and Nick Sonnenberg write that technology can optimize nearly any process that must be performed more than once.

We will consider four main categories of technology tools optimizing internal and external communications that an SFO should consider employing. These are: communication, collaboration, project management and task-specific tools.

A note about technology: It's important to understand the culture of the SFO, particularly its existing habits and workflows, before choosing to implement new technology tools. If half of your staff doesn't have a smartphone, asking them to use new technology will prove impossible and may actually leave you worse off. I encourage you to explore your options carefully; what works for one SFO won't necessarily work for yours. And, finally, technologies change rapidly. The descriptions in this chapter should be used as a jumping-off point for exploring technology solutions to pursue; please review any platform your SFO is considering before making a decision.

COMMUNICATION TECHNOLOGIES

Few among us would deny the importance of communication in an SFO—among the staff, to the board, to the generations of the family, with outside consultants—communication is key to an effective family office. Yet I see so many offices that rely on phone calls and emails to do business. We've come a long way from fax machines and phone calls, and even e-mail, for business communication. Modern tools offer instant connections with underlying organization and integrations that are designed for business rather than personal communication—both among colleagues and with customers or clients. Two of the current leaders in internal team communications are Slack and Skype. Both allow for instant messages, notifications, file sharing and even video messaging across a variety of devices (computer, tablet and smartphone). Slack has a casual interactive environment which allows the creation of teams; individuals can chat with one another or create topic- or project-related chat rooms in which all relevant members can participate. With over 1.25 million paid business users as of October 2016[9],

---

9 https://techcrunch.com/2016/10/20/slunk/

the company continues to offer new features in pursuit of growth and retention. Slack also prioritizes message encryption for added privacy. (The company does not store your messages on their servers in clear text.) Slack and Skype can provide useful ways to move topical conversations out of email and into a central, searchable location. They provide a great way to hold individuals accountable to the group for forward progress on deliverables.

Even Facebook and LinkedIn have made recent changes to their offerings to better allow for private communications among groups. Creating an invitation-only group on Facebook, where most individuals have existing accounts, can be an effective way to inform family members of SFO news and updates, foster conversations among the generations, and even welcome dialogue and feedback about operations and decisions. Many SFOs have turned to these existing social platforms as a way to avoid the cost of maintaining a private website. A word of caution, though: These sites do not offer secure communication and should not be used for sensitive information.

Tools that enable conversations between company and client, while potentially less relevant for SFOs, should be considered when there is a need to interact with a larger public. Families with public-facing brands might consider services like Intercom and Desk to manage customer service relations.

Other communications tools, like Twitter and Snapchat, typically don't align well with the needs of SFOs. Be wary of shifting to new communication tools before it's clear how established and secure they are.

COLLABORATION TECHNOLOGIES

SFOs are increasingly faced with a need to collaborate on projects with individuals spread across wide geographic areas. The days of paper and pencil products and face-to-face meetings are behind us. Luckily, digital collaboration with colleagues has never been easier. Tools like Dropbox, Google Docs, OneDrive and Quip allow for file sharing, document versioning, real-time editing by multiple parties, commenting and tracking changes. We can get buy-in and input from the SFO's various stakeholders by employing these tools.

Google offers the most comprehensive suite of Cloud applications, including Google Apps email and Drive file storage, Google Services for web hosting and Cloud storage (a competitor to Amazon's AWS), as well as Google Analytics and other tools.

If your SFO needs multiple services on that list, using a single provider for all of them has a huge upside. To date, Google has maintained the integrity of its security, not succumbing to the big data breaches we've see with other providers. However, the fact that they haven't had a problem before doesn't mean they won't in the future. Indeed, as we mentioned above, by using a Cloud provider for your documents, you are not only vulnerable to cyberattack, but possibly government subpoena of your Cloud-stored information without you being aware. So, before embracing an online service, consult with your legal advisors.

Bottom line: If you find your SFO sharing Word documents, spreadsheets, presentations or other projects back-and-forth over email, I strongly encourage some collaboration tool to make life easier for your staff.

PROJECT MANAGEMENT TECHNOLOGIES

Speaking of all those moving pieces—keeping track of all of them in a digital world can get complicated. Luckily, there are technology tools designed to do just that. Project management software allows you to create, define, assign, prioritize and track projects and their individual components. There is no shortage of technology tools in this bucket. Depending on your needs, some are better than others. If your SFO employs highly tech-savvy individuals who want deep capabilities and flexibility for customizations, using a PM tool like Basecamp or Redmine might be in order.

If, however, you find yourself in the boat that many SFOs do, you probably have a mixture of people with varying tech capabilities. In this case, a simpler, more user-friendly service is advisable. Trello is a personal favorite of mine for project management with a very low barrier to entry, a highly visual interface that is easy to understand, and deep integrations with other services, allowing for a cohesive approach to your communication and organizing. Trello's functionality closely mirrors to-do lists with individual items assigned to cards that can be moved between lists. New users can be on-boarded in minutes, but the service still allows for deeper capabilities for more advanced users.

Whichever project management tool your SFO chooses, simply capturing all your various projects, pieces and requirements in one place will allow you to see the big picture while simultaneously zooming in on the details. Effectively using a project management tool helps you ensure nothing falls through the cracks. Compare these centralized project boards to doing business via email chains or slips of paper on your desk—there is a clear winner, and it's digital.

These are just some of the technologies at our disposal today. In the early days of computers and the internet, learning a new piece of software was a full-time job. Today's technologies, however, are designed to be user-friendly and include quick on-boarding tutorials. With built-in help centers and customer support staff often available via live chat, it's hard to go wrong in choosing tools that will leapfrog your business communications and effectiveness. It is clear that SFOs should be looking to embrace technology to reduce staff burden, lower costs, and increase communication and effectiveness.

Conclusions

"Everything we hear is an opinion, not a fact. Everything we see is a perspective, not the truth. You have power over your mind—not outside events. Realize this, and you will find strength. Very little is needed to make a happy life; it is all within yourself, in your way of thinking."

—MARCUS AURELIUS, EMPEROR OF ROME FROM 161 TO 180

When it comes to dynastic wealth, families want their legacy, assets and resources to transition through the generations. Sustaining wealth can be invigorating because it allows family members to pursue their passions. Not everyone in the family will be an entrepreneur or great business leader. Some future family members will make wonderful teachers, artists or politicians, for example.

One possible danger in providing wealth to heirs is that it might kill motivation. Warren Buffet and Bill Gates have tried to avoid that danger by providing for their heirs' basic necessities, including medical care, education and housing, while earmarking the bulk of their estate while they're living, to philanthropic causes such as the Giving Pledge.

At the SFO level, however, families are in the stay-rich business. A world-class family office attempts to preserve wealth through careful tax management, wealth transfer planning, jurisdiction flexibility and ownership of generational assets. To remain generationally effective, the family office requires extraordinary leadership from the CEO down, with employees who have exceptional skills and character, are trustworthy, demonstrate grit, come from diverse backgrounds and are of widely varying ages in order to be "culturally additive."

Ideally, the SFO team should work with the family to develop a unified vision expressing the family's unique history, traditions and culture. The SFO delivers on the family's day-to-day needs and wants, and future financial, physical and digital security. It creates clear, transparent, and preferably collaborative, decision-making with the family, and focuses on the here and now, with an eye to the future.

These interesting times have amplified existing risks and created new ones, such as in the cyber realm, that pose a tremendous threat to wealth preservation. In many parts of the world, governments of the nations in which wealthy families reside present a significant risk to generational wealth preservation, such as lack of sustainable economic stability, runaway inflation, taxes and simply the power of governments to effectively do what they want. These threats continually up the ante in the game of wealth preservation. And yet, the vast majority of SFOs are woefully underprepared.

One ray of hope on the horizon is technology: AI, machine learning algorithms and VR. In the short-term, these innovations place additional resources at the fingertips of families and their SFOs. Those who know how to use these resources—sadly, that currently includes very few SFOs—can create opportunity to improve effectiveness.

Nevertheless, we cannot turn a blind eye to AI, machine learning algorithms, VR and robotics, as they could lead to massive unemployment and cause civil unrest and possibly chaos. There is no question that people will be affected, especially the less-educated and those who live in poverty. While we need to work together from a societal perspective to help with transitions in education and employment, a family and its SFO must understand what can go wrong and learn how to preserve wealth despite many risks.

In my work with global families of wealth, I have enjoyed the privilege of seeing some truly impressive, effective family offices. I have also seen the pitfalls endangering an SFO when all the pieces aren't properly aligned. It's important to understand the interplay of the ingredients covered in this book. It's not a single component that leads to success, but the continuous evaluation of your family office and constant improvement, that will help turn a mediocre family office into a world-class, high-performing one. From establishing a family's vision, to finding the right CEO and talent, to creating an enabling culture, the journey is a long, but not impossible, one. By establishing governance, embracing technology and opening an ongoing dialogue at all levels, you can create a truly effective family office.

My mission in writing this book has been to provide insights, tools and resources that enable wealthy families to create exceptional family offices that keep family members engaged, unified and able to work together to sustain the family's financial, social, emotional and spiritual wealth. It is my hope that this book will help many families meet these lofty, but achievable, goals. Resilience, adaptability, possessing the right resources and engaging people who truly understand these risks—these things have never been more important.

Some critical closing thoughts:

- Never lower the standards of your SFO.
- Always set your vision, goals, mission and standards high!
- Remain diligent, curious, open-minded and disciplined.

I wish you the best along this journey!

Bibliography

Antifragile: Things That Gain from Disorder, by Nassim Nicholas Taleb (Random House Trade Paperbacks, 2014)

Blockchain Revolution: How the Technology Behind Bitcoin is Changing Money, Business and the World, by Don and Alex Tapscott (Portfolio, 2016)

The Brand Gap: How to Bridge the Distance between Business Strategy and Design, by Marty Neumeier (New Riders; revised and expanded edition, 2006)

Built to Last: Successful Habits of Visionary Companies, by Jim Collins (HarperBusiness, 2004)

Clued In: How to Keep Customers Coming Back Again and Again, by Lou Carbone (FT Press, 2004)

Drive: The Surprising Truth About What Motivates Us, by Daniel H. Pink (the LatestEdition, 2009)

The Effective Executive: The Definitive Guide to Getting the Right Things Done, by Peter F. Drucker, with new foreword by Jim Collins (HarperBusiness, 2017)

The Extraordinary Leader: Turning Good Managers into Great Leaders, by John Zenger and Joseph Folkman (McGraw Hill Education, 2009)

Family Wealth: Keeping It in the Family, by James E. Hughes Jr. (Bloomberg Press, 2004)

The Founder's Mentality: How to Overcome the Predictable Crises of Growth, by Chris Zook and James Allen (Harvard Business Review Press, 2016)

Give and Take: A Revolutionary Approach to Success, by Adam Grant (Viking, April 2013)

Good to Great: Why Some Companies Make the Leap...And Others Don't, by Jim Collins (HarperBusiness, 2001)

Grit: The Power of Passion and Perseverance by Angela Duckworth (Scribner, 2016)

Idea to Execution: How to Optimize, Automate and Outsource Everything in Your Business, by Ari Meisel and Nick Sonnenberg (Lioncrest Publishing, 2016)

The Inevitable: Understanding the 12 Technological Forces That Will Shape Our Future, by Kevin Kelly (Viking, 2016)

Leadership is an Art, by Max Dupree (Doubleday, 2004)

Mindset: The New Psychology of Success, by Carol S. Dweck (Ballantine Books, 2007)

Resilience Thinking: Sustaining Ecosystems and People in a Changing World, by David Salt and Brian Walker (Island Press, 2006)

The Road to Ruin: The Global Elites' Secret Plan for the Next Financial Crisis, by James Rickards (Portfolio, 2016)

Peter Drucker's Five Most Important Questions: Enduring Wisdom for Today's Leaders by Peter Drucker, Frances Hesselbein and Joan Snyder Kuhl (Jossey-Bass, 2015)

Team of Teams: New Rules of Engagement for a Complex World, by General Stanley McChrystal, Tantum Collins, David Silverman, Chris Fussell (Portfolio, 2015)

Tools of Titans: The Tactics, Routines, and Habits of Billionaires, Icons, and World-Class Performers, by Tim Ferriss (Houghton Mifflin Harcourt, 2016)

Turn the Ship Around: The True Story of Turning Followers into Leaders, by L. David Marquet (Portfolio, 2013)

Who: The A Method for Hiring by Geoff Smart and Randy Street (Ballantine Books, 2008

Appendix: The Most Common SFO Services

There are hundreds of services that can fall under the primary areas of the SFO services listed in this section. The obligation of the family is to identify which services it expects and demands from the SFO.

The SFO must to provide these services and proactively recommend other services it can perform, and service the family excellently.

Because some services fall under multiple primary areas, an effective SFO must understand the interconnectivity between one service and another and how to integrate services harmoniously.

SFOs do not necessarily need to execute, deliver or even manage all of the services the family desires. Some, if not many, may remain the domain of outsourced providers. Services the family office may provide directly include:

WEALTH PRESERVATION

- Mitigate and manage portfolio risks
- Understand and, where needed, hedge varying exposures
- Carefully manage all global banking, brokerage and custodial relationships
- Carefully manage physical ownership of gold, silver, art and jewels as part of a diverse allocation focused on generational wealth preservation
- Understand the value of strategically global land and farmland ownership as a generational wealth preservation asset
- Coordinate investment decisions carefully with tax considerations
- Evaluate purchasing leverage, fee minimization and cost savings opportunities
- Provide exceptional knowledge, resources and coordination of advanced tax, estate and asset-protection strategies
- Manage digital/cyber risks with world-class resources
- Monitor global geopolitical risks, which can change from year to year
- Maintain banking and custodial relationships for cash, safety deposit boxes, public equities, and business connections and resources in varying countries (possibly including the United States, Canada, New Zealand, Switzerland, Australia, Singapore and Malta)

- Refuse rehypothecation of your brokerage accounts—most commonly, by not opening a margin account (some brokerages add margin accounts by default.)
- Maintain sufficient cash and currencies in varied global non-banking locations
- Conduct annual due diligence on domestic and foreign banks, brokerages and custodians, focusing on their financials and cyber-security measures
- Diversify global locations (including non-bank) of gold, silver and jewels

ASSET PROTECTION

- Conduct investment due diligence
- Provide and regularly evaluate insurance services
- Hire, perform background checks on, and manage household, business and family office staff
- Provide reputation management
- Evaluate personal security, privacy and confidentiality services
- Coordinate tax, estate and asset-protection plans; changes and recommendations of legal domicile; and citizenship of family members and beneficiaries
- Proactively manage, coordinate and update trusts and other legal entities, as applicable, per changes in family member domicile, citizenship, marital status, births and deaths, etc.
- Coordinate most the effective ownership structure of assets per family goals and tax considerations
- Coordinate with outside counsel any changes in family member domicile or citizenship, and the impact of state and country regulations and laws since last reviewed
- Review latest strategies, including conversations with world-class professionals, to further secure family assets

RISK MANAGEMENT

- Clearly understand all the family's cash, equity and fixed-income assets and use analytical resources to assess risks

- Manage custodial risks on cash and public equity holdings
- Manage currency exposure
- Analyze and update all LP and non-controlling interests for fraud, style drift and other manager risks
- Diversify and monitor all global banking and brokerage relationships
- Monitor geopolitical risks of countries where family members live, visit, and hold or invest in resources
- Clearly understand and maintain privacy policies of all provider services and investment managers
- Review the online security protocols of all providers
- Review and re-evaluate insurance and all exposures
- Update all liability umbrella insurance policies
- Consider the costs and benefits of E&O and D&O insurance
- Manage the health insurance exposures of family members
- Ensure that the family's luxury assets (such as aircraft, boats, jewels, art, etc.) are properly insured
- Consider a captive insurer and its potential tax and asset protection benefits
- Review social media protocols with family and SFO staff
- Ensure SFO's diligent adherence to password protocols
- Manage ALL digital and cyber threats

INVESTMENT SERVICES

- Develop and adapt an investment policy statement
- Develop and adapt an asset allocation strategy
- Source and update diligence on direct investments
- Source and update diligence on portfolio managers as an LP investor
- Be aware of leverage
- Ensure all investment management and advisory fees are completely and radically transparent
- Provide aggregation of and reporting on all assets
- Consider impact investments

- Set performance to benchmarks and expectations, compared with exceptionally liquid, transparent and tax-efficient passive options
- Manage aviation and yacht assets, including for maximum tax benefits
- Coordinate family art services
- Review and coordinate cash management services
- Consider and correct ownership structure and management of domestic and global land and art
- Keep up to date with digital currencies such as Bitcoin and Blockchain technology

DISASTER AND TRAVEL PLANNING

- Monitor countries with flexible corporate and trust laws for the transfer of U.S.-based assets
- Create and regularly update disaster plans for evacuation of the family, along with its aviation pilot and his/her family
- Manage family communication protocols and various methods of global coordination and communication (including satellite phones), and conduct practice drills in the event of varying disasters
- Manage server and online risks including back-ups
- Manage family reputation and discretion
- Update passports for family
- Consider dual or multiple citizenship in various countries
- Consider preparing to obtain dual citizenship that allows freedom to travel internationally. Check for jurisdictions that participate in the USA Visa Waiver Program. Determine countries family members will live in or travel to and check whether visa is required for entry
- Prepare a plan for obtaining visas for entering the United States (as applicable)
- Check that yacht ownership and registration (the flag of yacht) are offshore and research which ports of entry allow for ease of travel and entry
- Be aware of rules regarding entry to the United States by foreigners on foreign-owned and registered aircraft. If future entry to the U.S. is contemplated, the entity that operates the aircraft can be an American entity leasing the aircraft from the foreign owner

- Investigate foreign concierge medical practices for health care outside the United States (This is still rare outside the United States, except in Geneva, Zurich and London.)
- Investigate proactive family initiatives, including philanthropies, to maintain society and civil order
- Add new and maintain current family and business political connections globally

COMPLEX ASSETS MANAGEMENT

- Residential real estate
- Commercial real estate
- Operating businesses
- Collections
- Sports teams
- Socially responsible investments

ACCOUNTING, TAX PLANNING AND COMPLIANCE

- Accounting and tax filings
- Identify and engage outsourced providers
- Develop and coordinate estate plans for all family members
- Implement and administer trusts
- Consider a private trust company
- Provide proactive and strategic tax plans
- Analyze complex tax depreciation, wealth transfer pricing and other advanced tax planning strategies for assets
- Consider becoming a strategic global citizen in countries that offer exceptional tax benefits and allow citizenship without true residency
- Coordinate tax planning with wealth transfer, estate planning and asset protection
- Analyze and manage tax exposure of investments
- Coordinate tax services with outsourced tax counsel

- Create an SFO tax committee
- File taxes for trust and corporate entities, as applicable
- Administer private trust company
- Review from tax perspective all trusts, legal and corporate entities, and partnerships. Investigate how arbitrage might be improved by a change of situs, ownership, gifting, etc.

ESTATE PLANNING

- Review and update, as applicable, wills of family members
- Review and coordinate updates, as applicable, of trusts and legal and corporate entities, especially after marriages, divorces, births and deaths of family members
- Coordinate with outside counsel trusts and gifting opportunities with interest rates, intra-family loans and other changes in governmental rates
- Review appraisals and value of assets and consider proactive plans for gifting and intra-family loans, depending on increases and decreases of assets
- Update existing plans in the event of family member death or disability, including incapacity
- Have elder care planning strategy in place for aging family members
- Explore further gifting opportunities
- Provide prenuptial agreements as applicable
- Review all illiquid, non-voting interests
- Review situs of trusts for maximum benefits
- Review trustees of all trusts
- Create or update trust summaries for all trusts
- Update any guardianship documents, as well as power of attorney, health proxies and HIPAA privacy release forms for all family members

FAMILY SERVICES

- Consider creating a family bank and intra-family loan programs
- Guide and assist where possible in family communication, harmony and process to decision-making (governance)

- Monitor philanthropy and charitable activities
- Create or regularly update the family mission, constitution and governance
- Align family legacy, vision and values
- Educate and engage the next generation
- Organize family retreats
- Manage and monitor family members' medical needs
- Evaluate and implement personal and property security systems and procedures
- Provide concierge services (travel planning, private aviation, personal shopping)
- Report to family any changes in assets and resources
- Assist with family charity and philanthropic endeavors
- Coordinate personal security services
- Coordinate family travel and concierge services
- Provide health and medical management and services
- Manage household staffing
- Coordinate family property construction and remodeling projects
- Manage aviation and yacht staffing
- Assist with and coordinate services to help family members with mental disorders or addictions
- Organize and update family members' passports
- Manage family member distributions of capital
- Coordinate and monitor intra-family loans

FAMILY OFFICE MANAGEMENT

- Understand the family's mission, vision and goals for the SFO, and check regularly that the family office is meeting them effectively
- Update or redefine the SFO vision and mission statement
- Challenge the SFO to "think big"
- Provide for continuing education, opportunity and resources for the CEO and other managers to improve their effectiveness, resilience and adaptability
- Evaluate SFO employees' and the resources they need to succeed

- Review with the family and HR any additions, subtractions or status quo of the SFO employees' needs
- Initiate or evaluate the value of SFO committees (tax, comp, etc.)
- Maintain consistent communication with family chairman and rising family members
- Educate rising family members about finance
- Review and update SFO employee manuals and training protocols
- Update employee NDAs and employee agreements
- Conduct employee performance valuations
- Review employee compensation
- Manage and enhance the evolving the SFO culture
- Monitor how family members perceive the SFO brand
- Maintain protocol of key family member contact information, including via social media
- Conduct fire drills for "White Knight Hacking" of the SFO and take other security measures
- Solicit feedback about how the family feels about the SFO's success and what can be improved
- Evaluate ALL outside vendors
- Create and regularly evaluate and improve the CEO's succession plan
- Hire successful integrated interns
- Experiment with disrupting aspects of the SFO's business and services, possibly using interns
- Network regularly with world-class SFOs and learn from them

Acknowledgments

I'd like to take a moment and acknowledge some wonderful people without whose conversations, opinions and considerations this book would not have been possible. I am incredibly grateful for the following: The loving support and encouragement of my wife Maria and my family, including Dylan, Starsky and Fritzie. My co-author of the "Creating an SFO" white paper, Amy Renkert-Thomas. The creative thoughts regarding leadership, culture and brand from Dana Green, John Wong and Matt Wesley. The global perspective and eloquent wordsmithing of my friend Marc Halsema. Thoughts and guidance on defining the successful family office workplace of Lyn Christensen. Compensation expertise of Trish Botoff. The awareness of a global citizenship perspective of John Prescott. The creative mindset and youthful perspective of Ryan Ansin. The immense value of the legal perspectives in thinking beyond the box of friends Joe Field, Scott Beach, Tom Handler and David Berek. Insights on the tax perspective by Paul Morelli. Thoughts on family and family office interaction and harmony of Jay Hughes, Kirby Rosplock, Barbara Hauser, Dennis Jaffe, Jim Grubman, Fredda Herz-Brown and Patricia Angus. Writing and technology perspective of Marcie Braden and the superlative writing and editing of Jayne Pearl.

In reality there are hundreds of amazing people I've been fortunate to meet over the years, individuals, family office executives, advisors and thought leaders who were all influential in defining my thinking and thoughts on the family office community. It truly takes a village. I wish to thank them all, too numerous to list; however, their contributions are forever valued and cherished.

About Angelo J. Robles

Angelo Robles is founder and CEO of the Greenwich, Conn.-based Family Office Association (FOA), one of the world's largest and most exclusive global membership organizations dedicated to families of exceptional success and their single family offices.

Additionally, as the founder of data-driven Family Office Statistics, founder of the family office think tank Effective Family Office, and author of his book by the same name, Robles's expertise is often sought by media outlets such as Bloomberg Television, *Forbes*, the *Wall Street Journal*, *Institutional Investor* and others. Robles continues to lead in the single family office community with creative thinking on the future of the family office via proprietary research, original writing, masterclasses and workshops, global programming and his regular podcast, *Angelo Robles's Effective Family Office Podcast* on iTunes. Additionally, Robles personally advises a small number of global families and single family office executives on achieving maximum effectiveness.

In servicing a community historically limited in its use of transformative and creative best practices and beyond-the-box thinking, Robles is radically redefining family offices globally by converging effectiveness, resiliency and adaptiveness with improving results in the single family office.

Robles helps educate, position and provide resources to families, family office executives and those who serve the community in being prepared and extraordinary.

Contact Angelo Robles:
familyofficeassociation.com
effectivefamilyoffice.com
angelo@familyofficeassociation.com
angelo@angelorobles.com
(203) 570-2898
Follow on Twitter @familyoffice

Sign up for the *Effective Family Office Podcast* on iTunes, iHeart or Stitcher today.